ARRIVAL PRESS

SPRING IS IN THE AIR

Edited

By

TIM SHARP

First published in Great Britain in 1996 by
ARRIVAL PRESS
1 - 2 Wainman Road, Woodston,
Peterborough, PE2 7BU

HB ISBN 1 85786 482 4
SB ISBN 1 85786 477 8

Foreword

The writers included in this wonderful collection delve deep into their creativity to share their feelings on the magical season of spring.

Poems range from the start of new life to new loves and relationships that the writers have experienced.

Editing this anthology was especially difficult as the standard and quantity of poetry received was outstanding.

I hope the final selection brings joy to all those who read it as the collection was a delight to put together.

Tim Sharp
Editor

CONTENTS

A SPRING MESSAGE

Coldness and darkness loomed everywhere
With dreary days that spelt despair,
Nature so barren, lay silently asleep
Whilst winter gales roared, and snow lay deep.

Hibernating like animals, humans wistfully would try,
Snuggled up in their beds, they would silently lie.
Till morning sunbeams shone, bidding everyone *arise*!
With the *spring message* of *awakening* - a joyous surprise!

As newborn chicks popped out of their shell,
Humans would feel reborn 'neath this springtime spell.
New life, new energy, bursts of spring cleaning too,
And clocks go *on* one hour, for more daylight for you.

This *spring message* is magic, it awakens everything,
Baby bunnies, skipping lambs, are born to greet the spring,
Trees' green buds are sprouting, everything is fresh and new,
The unspoken *spring message* happens yearly, it's strange but true!

High up in the trees, love songs birds will sing,
Young couples pounding heartbeats, bring love ties and a ring.
Snowdrops, cowslips, daffodils and tulips too,
A glorious colourful rainbow, will fill gardens for all to view.

Gone are the days, when we crept in and out of the dark,
Now we'll walk with a spring and rise with the lark.
It's goodbye to darkness, the *light* and *joy* are here,
With Easter greetings, celebrations, gives *thanks* and a *cheer*!

Stella Bush-Payne

TIME'S GREAT TIDE OF SEASON

How shall I write I love her
for nature as if so designed
awakes a wild elation and -
spring's playful in my mind.

For time's great tide of season
sweeps through me like a mood
like opening of daffodils
or spinning of the moon.

I knew not how to tell her
nor how to summarise
so I captured spring's inheritance
of warmth and crimson skies.

I looked for inspiration
in every grace of flower
I saw her sparkle in the dew,
her freshness in each shower.

When at last I looked no more
my love to her was bidden
but time's great tide of season turned
and where was my love hidden?

Ben Cook

TWILIGHT OVER THE DAWN

Day breaks, morning awakes
The bees in the trees make honey
Dew drops sparkle as life begins
Dawn gave life to all around

Over the hills, over the dales,
Echoes of laughter re-echoed their sounds
Tears of happiness to all around

The heaven in all its splendour
Breathing the air awakening like the dawn
Silver clouds casting shadows
The lark in the sky answers to echoes from the ground

Twilight comes, twilight fades
The dawn, the day, the night depends
Life was passed and over awaiting yet another day.

Joseph Mitchell

IF I SAID I LOVE YOU FIONA

If I said I love you until the end of time,
Would you say that you would be mine?

If I said I love you for your personality and wit,
Would you say that you love me as I do you to bits?

If I said I love you when so close to me you are near,
Would you want to come and stay with me forever here?

If I said I love you so much you always make me feel good,
Would you let me make you happy the way that I should?

If I said I love you with all of my heart,
Would you come and stay with me, never ever wanting to part?

If I said I love you as I have loved none other,
Would you come back and always be my lover?

If I said I love you for the way you make love and kiss,
Would you say this is the same about me right now, you miss?

If I said I love you when we cuddle tight and kiss,
Would you say right now you to this you also miss?

If I said I love the feeling of your beautiful soft smooth skin,
Would you say you'd want me right now to hold you tight within?

Patrick J D Gray

AN OLD FLAME

An opportunity was put before me
But I was too blind to see
It was just today
When I was walking home the usual way

Whilst walking under the bridge, I saw an old flame
And my feelings for him are still the same
We smiled, said hello, and he asked how I was
I said 'Fine', and then felt very cross
This is because I just walked away
With very little to say

I am now lying on my bedroom floor
Wishing so much that I had said more
I have all these thoughts in my head
Of the things I could have said

I'll just have to wait till the next time I see him
And then hopefully I will have thought of something
He probably thinks I don't like him any more
But I have done, for three years or four.

Lena M Sheach

THE SEA

I've always liked the sea
As long as I can tell
It really makes me feel good
I even like the smell

Its special fascination
That never goes away
I'd love to live close by it
Instead of going for the day

I prefer the sea to swim in
As the salt helps you to float
The waves bring added pleasure
Or you can go out in a boat

I'm hoping to go back this summer
With the person I adore
He shares my enthusiasm
So we might go more and more

Susan Edwards

THE COMING OF SPRING

The valley and hills,
And a clear sky blue lake,
Floating marshmallow clouds
Leaving the sunshine in their wake.

The trees whistle in silent winds,
Branching out to greet the beckoning sunshine,
The valleys covered in rich lavender,
And the birds whistle at beauty so fine.

Dew hangs lazily on moistened leaves,
Glistening in the early morning sun,
Spiders create their own webs of intrigue
Which were woven before time began.

And finally spring has arrived,
No longer the frosted earth,
And chilling winds,
Just the beauty of nature's rebirth.

Jeremy C W Bloomfield

THE GARDENER'S ODE TO SPRING

Spring arrived this morning, at the very crack of dawn,
With cockroaches and beetles, leather jackets for the lawn.
Ground elder, dock and dandelion are coming on a pace,
Flea beetles making radish leaves resemble Brussels lace.
A flock of ravenous pigeons have alighted on the greens,
And a postcard from 'Down Under' said they've found my runner beans.
My onion sets all stood in line, till sparrows came to play,
Now they're scattered round the garden, in a state of disarray.
The broad beans, only yesterday, were green from base to tips,
Now they're blackened by the black fly, as the aphids smack their lips.
The brown ale in the saucer should have killed the snails and slugs,
But it seems they've had a 'knees-up', with the wire worms and the bugs.
And hungry mice, who watched me as I sowed the early peas,
Are gorging with their 'cronies', what a blow out, if you please.
Well the greenhouse won't need whitewash on its roof, or down the sides,
A family of wood pigeons very kindly have obliged.
But spring arrived this morning, not with song, but desperate shouts,
As I watched the neighbour's cat defile my row of Brussels sprouts.

Hilda Jones

IT'S SPRING

The long dark nights of winter has passed.
Ice, snow, bitter winds that blow are ceased.
Grass is turning from brown to green.
It's spring and the world's full of music.
Birds in the trees, and hedges sing,
'Wake up. Wake up,
It's spring. It's spring.'

'It's spring and a fresh breeze blows'
The warm sun shines upon the earth.
And in the gardens, the flowers begin to grow.
Birds in their nests hatch out their eggs.
Spring lambs frolic and skip in the fields,
Young lovers walk hand in hand through the long grass.
Hearts are filled with love and joy.
'Because it's spring. It's spring.'

Doreen Petherick Cox

EDEN

History began in a garden
That Eden oh so fair
Where God strolled with Adam
Enjoying the evening air
And God saw Adam was lonely
And needed company
So, He formed Eve, while Adam slept
Creating humanity
Then sin came into Eden, and Satan
The master of sin
Encircled Eve by persuasion
And Eve believed him
God was very angry, but let the devil have his way
So that is how sin came into the world today
Remember, when you are tempted
Try not to give in, wear your faith as your shield
The victory to win

Bunty Hardman

LAVATERA MANOR

What troubles thee my sweet butterfly
With your torn at silken wings
No longer the sweet song of lullabies
Your resident angels sing
Rather the pre-metamorphosis returns
When you lived with your relative worms
What troubles thee my sweet butterfly
Your tears soak painfully my soul
What is it that makes you cry
That turns to ash your heart of gold

Sorcerer deals at the round table
Another hard day for his slaves
She's nothing but an untamed shrew
We're nothing but ravens and knaves

What troubles thee my sweet Lavatera
With your song of strong concern
I'll be climbing up later to hear you
The new horizon I strongly yearn
Rather the gold sunset of tomorrow
When be gone this night of sorrow
What troubles thee my sweet girl
We're soon to escape from here
Give my life for your new world
Sweet butterfly flower don't you fear

Rodger Moir

LOVE

When love is in its infant days
And youth is on your side
It's full of fun and joyfulness
Your excitement you can't hide

And as your years accelerate
Couples with eyes devouring
His body develops to manhood
Your womanliness is flowering

Your joy of him just grows and grows
Until he takes your breath away
And your heartbeat becomes much faster
With every passing day

The newness of your love together
Is full of warmth and desire
You feel your body will explode
If your feelings run much higher

And as the years go passing by
And you're busy building your life
It's sometimes hard to remember
How long you've been man and wife

But when you reflect on your youthful days
With a passion with no end
You can rejoice in the fact you have now both
A lover and a friend

Jean McDonnell

SPRING

Spring stirs;
the earth rolls over and purrs
beneath the plough.

Shafted beams
caress reluctant seams
of dormant buds.

Showers embrace
warming abundant greenness to chase
cool winter shades.

Rainbow colours
renew the promise in flowers
of consummation.

Hills and valleys
echo with songs and sounds to seize
the waiting senses.

Spring wakes;
the nascent world celebrates
its re-creation.

Shirley Johnson

THE RETURN OF SPRING

On a dark winter's day twelve years ago
I lost the love of my young life,
After sixteen years of laughter and love,
A widow, no longer a wife.

It seemed that spring would never come again,
But time, the healer, set me free.
This year, as the spring flowers put forth bloom,
Love blossomed once again for me.

'Nice that you've found companionship,' said some.
I nodded, laughing in my heart,
For this new loving joyful is, and fierce,
No autumn romance, a fresh start.

Passionate, warming, tender, all at once,
Bright gold, like my new wedding ring.
No muted tones of dull October days,
But sap-filled, flaunting shades of spring.

Liz Glen

MY SPRINGTIME LOVE

Whenever April ends
And spring comes around
My mind always strays
To a time we spent together
In that spring of yesterday
It was such a lovely feeling
Everything new was in the air
I felt as though I had been reborn
Not a worry or a care

We would go for walks
In that early spring
My life was right and new
I could face up to anything
As long as I was with you
The daffodils, the little lambs
Whenever spring comes round
Always take me back
To that time we had
And the true love I had found.

Christine Williams

SPRING IS IN THE AIR

My darling, when spring is in the air, I think of love.
I love you with all my heart.
My one and only turtle-dove, I hope we never ever part.
What more can I say? A little love goes a long way!

The more you love me, the more I love you
And my love for you grows and grows.
The way you make me happy, with your love deep and true,
The happiness in me shows and shows.
What more can I say? A little love goes a long way!

When I kiss you gently, the love-light shows in your eyes.
When sometimes you've caught me crying, you look at me with surprise.
For all that your love yields - my every need supplies.
What more can I say? A little love goes a long, long way!

When I'm with you, my feelings are very strong.
And when I'm away from you, I often cry.
If you ever leave me - don't let it be for long.
I know I'll be so lonely - I could even die!
What more can I say? A little love goes a long way.

These words to you, are not *just* words - but by way of a plea.
Oh please, oh please, don't take away your love, but take me
To your heart - and take me away with thee!
What more can I say? A little love does - go a long way.

Sally Branson

NEWBORN SPRING

Exclusively ours, in spring of '88.
Our love in our new home.
Was it to be our fate?

Do you remember the daffodils
Displayed in our new garden?
Our lives were soft and innocent,
But fate would make us harden.

We cleared away the cobwebs
Of whose memories shared the past.
In this new time we blossomed,
But the blossom failed to last.

Laughter, tears and sadness,
We learned by our mistakes.
And no-one every told us
That our dream would soon awake.

Now spring of '96 is here,
And we are that much older.
The warmth has rekindled in our hearts,
Though this spring is much colder.

And as we step away from all,
We turn our heads to see
The daffodils still growing
Underneath the blossom tree.

Another chapter over,
Another to begin.
And my love we're still together
To share our newborn spring.

Amanda Bayes

SO BEAUTIFUL

So beautiful the trees in leaf.
So tall, so grand, so green.
I look around me as I walk,
Such beauty to be seen.

I strolled across the park today
And I felt the quiet sway.
The leaves danced gaily in the breeze
And my thoughts did go astray.
. . . So beautiful, the trees in May.

Pamela M Lannon

SECRET DOOR

In my mind's eye, crystal clear
Is a magical castle, not far from here,
Where dreams come alive, no wish too small,
Just close your eyes, you can have it all.

Walking through the gardens with love on your mind,
Winter hath gone, summer graces the sky,
Soft green grass beneath your toes,
Warm summer breezes all around you blow.

Bringing the sweet scent of flowers your way,
The scene is set for a beautiful day,
Lost in your dreams of a fantasy play,
A prince touches your face in a tender way.

He brings his lips closer till you touch with a kiss,
Making you tingle with heavenly bliss,
What do you wish now, what are you feeling for?
Only you hold the key to your secret door.

Christine Nicholson

SPRING IS IN THE AIR

Yes spring is in the air,
And love is everywhere,
Blossom on trees both red and white
Makes a really wonderful sight.

Yes spring is in the air,
Cob and pen, still a pair,
Swim around and do their best
To build this year another nest.

Yes spring is in the air,
The cuckoo's over there,
The swallows and the swifts return,
Maypole dances in school we learn.

Yes spring is in the air,
See rabbit and the hare,
Who play at dusk above the ground
But scamper at the slightest sound.

Yes spring is in the air,
And would you really dare?
Use an old tree rope for a swing,
Yes of course you would in spring.

Yes spring is in the air,
Again we have the fair,
Which settles on the village green,
With stalls and rides there to be seen.

Yes spring is in the air,
Young people give no care
To all the warning from their mum,
No harm to them could ever come!

Catherine Craft

SPRING (PERSEPHONE)

Spring! She is the season in two parts
The growing seed - the purest heart,
The vital grain that ever feeds
The earth and all mankind now needs.

Alive and potent, yet so mild
She gently nurtures nature's child
The corn, the wheat, the fruit and flowers,
She endows with all her powers.

Yet! Soon she will just fade away
Deep underground her part to play,
She procreates with every breath
Goddess of generation and death!

Mavis Johnson

SPRING IS IN THE AIR

The trees are slowly coming into bloom,
The scent of blossom fills the room.
The garden is living, again back to show,
Beauty and wonder makes my heart glow.

No more frosts for a month or two,
Lighter evenings are now on cue.
Lambs are running about in the grass,
Sunlight mornings will come to pass.

How wonderful to see the grass so green,
Such beautiful shades for the eye to be seen.
A colourful season to show such flair,
Now once more spring is in the air.

Fran Zubek

APRIL GIRLS

As if, from winter, were cocooned,
Then into spring's young light released,
In season's throat, new voices, tuned,
And, as nature, only in warmth, increased,
April girls came walking by,
Are painted in the palest way,
Lost instances, to multiply;
What point? To be beside their youth to say,
Of blunt and rusty razor blades;
Perhaps a 'Sixties' dance or two,
With the scent of top-shelf aftershave'
Reincarnation: by far the best for you,
Than many things no longer there;
For second-likeness (safe is seed)
Creates you, quite a millionaire;
Few coppers wealth is all she needs
For young adventures to the store;
Of father's stance and mother's curls,
Heart's multiples are churned the more,
In her dance amongst the April girls.

Large-bowed and long is Easter dress,
And if affinity brings a scare,
Then you are suitably impressed,
Bend back and knee, to childhood things down there;
Where, perhaps, a grass-held song,
Or the face beside some flame you blew,
Or the features that in clouds belong,
Bring April girls back home to you.

W Sutch

SPRING OF THE HEART

Oh Lady Spring how beautiful art thou,
the beaming celandines bedeck
thy gown and now the speedwell
scatters her fairy dust there,
upon the shining tresses of thy hair.
Would that my heart could ever share
thy sensuous beauty and enchantment,
but the cold winds of despair
blight the tender blossoms of the
frail canopy of love and I cannot repair
its tender flowers again.

Pat Watson

A COOL PINT

Candlelight
reflects eyes
in the eyes of my lover,
a triangle on the floor;
carpet gold.
My tongue
glides over her silken head
leaving a cleft
of pure delight,
embracing as I watch
the frost on her silica skin,
I lift her open mouth
to mine
and
kiss.

Benjamin F Jones

ZING IT'S SPRING

I am longing for spring.
To hear the birds sing.
Winter's a long time going,
The snowdrop not yet showing.
Suddenly you see it's here,
The snowdrops are out, cheer!
Daffodils, primroses, bluebells too,
What does it do to you?
Blossoms of pink and white,
Oh! Such a lovely sight.
Spring is subtle and real
Offering you a new deal
Time to think and review
You are a wonder too.
New young lives are beginning
Your heart is a'singing.
Just guess who I've seen!
The man of my dream.
My heart is a flutter,
I'm all of a stutter,
He's walking over this way,
What's he going to say!
The doorbell ring rings.
His arms full with things.
Hello! Is this number four?
I'm Tim from next door.
here's your parcels and letter,
Please take, they're getting wetter.
I hope we meet again,
I'm departing from the rain.

Muriel Spencer

LOVE IN MAY

The hedges of hawthorn are heavy with may,
And the grass has grown high, green and sweet.
Sun on the river makes splashes of light,
And I lift up my face to its heat.

And I lift up my face to your love,
To a wild and a breathless beginning.
Oh the light in your eyes and the heat of the day
And my spirit is dancing and spinning!

The blue sky is open, forever to space
And the springtime is bursting with life.
Oh this wonderful May! Will we still feel this way
When we become husband and wife?

Irena Kirton

LOVE ETERNAL

Words of love from you
are nought compared to the feelings that do run deep
in the hearts of Lee and Sue.

Forever more their love they shall have to keep
from the break of day
until they lay down to sleep.

Ask of them whatever you may
anything but their love can be yours
for neither shall ever stray.

In their lives there be one true cause
something for which they're willing to pay any fee
break down any obstacles, any doors.

As forever together, they must be
eternal lovers, Sue and Lee.

Phil Dee

YOU

Everywhere I turn you are not there.
At night I lie awake and find no place
Your shadow does not curve. It hurts
All over, and yet no doctor could translate the pain,
Or find a healing for the loss
That will not go away.

Kenneth C Steven

WATCH THE BIRDIE!

The spring is sprung, I've had a twinge,
It's time I stopped the booze and binge,
It's time I tried to dine and date,
It's time I found myself a mate.

The spring is sprung, and marriage calls,
Who needs the darts and snooker halls?
Who cares the odds are ten to four?
Who wants to know the rugby score?

The spring is sprung, it's birds and bees,
Begone fast cars and dungarees,
Begone the gambling in the club,
Begone the punch-up in the pub.

The spring is sprung, and then in lieu
Of match, ten pints and Vindaloo,
We'll watch TV and knock Madonna
And sleep in front of Des O'Connor.

The spring is sprung, it's getting late,
And so I've found myself a mate,
For in the end, come rain or shine,
Us girls - we have to toe the line!

Dave E Priest

SPRING!

Once again spring is with us
There is beauty all around,
The birds fly above us
Life is stirring on the ground!
This has been a cold start
For this season of the year,
When the warm blood in our hearts
Begins to stir both hope and fear!
Young love disturbs us!
Too shy to make a move
We see the one we yearn for
Blissfully ignorant of our love!
We must overcome that shyness
Maybe ask a friend
Or even a sister to oblige us,
Our misery to end!
Joy at last! It's over!
We are together now,
Our love will last for ever
That shall be my vow!

It was not a sister
Nor a friend to help one out
Just a sunblind proving awkward
Needing a gentle clout!

Claude A Knight

MY HUSBAND - THE SOLDIER

You are my life and best friend too
I love you heaps, I really do.
We always seem so far apart
But deep inside you fill my heart.

You always make me smile so much
In private, in public, I love your touch.
You really mean the world to me
Without you, I don't want to see.

I always cope while you're away
But in my mind you always stay
A few miles here, a few miles there,
I sense you round me everywhere.

For these ten years we've been a pair
We row, we laugh, we've had despair
And 'cos we love each other so
The bond between us will ever grow.

I love you so with all my power
Every day, each passing hour
We'll stay together as husband and wife
Until we leave this present life.

Thanks my love, for being you
Your daughters and I respect you too.
We know you're worth your weight in gold
Come home safe, you're wanted to hold.

Happy 10th Anniversary Steve.

M A Commander

AND SO IT IS

If only it were that I did not care
That spring is in the air
That I could eat and drink and love
The stars away
Knowing that your love will stay
But life is life
And sunshine is always
Followed by cloud
And baptismal gown by shroud
But let the interim go not unlived
And let the sweet perfume of spring
Be celebrated to the full.

Clive Cornwall

ONLY YOU ARE THERE

You feed my soul with something I don't fear
You listen to my words, what I say you hear
You take control when I need you more
You set me right when I'm not sure
You love me more than anyone can
I see you are no match for another man
My heart it aches when you're not here
But a phone call away and you're so near
You question nothing I do or say
You judge me not in any way
You're able to make my dreams so real
You know what I need, you know how I feel

You ask for no thank-yous, I need not say sorry
You never possess, you just set me free
And when I stumble and fall in life
You're there in an instant to take away the strife

Jacqui Simpkin

WHAT SPRING MEANS TO ME

Spring is here, you can feel it in the air,
With new baby lambs prancing everywhere.
They run and play and jump into the air,
They're having fun without a care.
Blooming flowers, chirping birds,
Are there for all to see,
Time for romance, time for love,
That's what spring means to me.

Marie Louise Wainwright (12)

SAY IT WITH ROSES

I grow these roses for you each day,
'But you have no garden,' I hear you say:
Well, they are from the garden within my heart
And as I pick each bunch I hope we will never part.

I tend them daily, I hope not in vain,
I shower them with love, instead of rain,
And as I watch each flower bloom,
I hope you will be mine, forever - soon.

In my garden there's no frost or snow,
And the cold winds from the north will never blow,
But there's lots of sunshine, laughter too,
For the flowers I grow remind me of you.

And as the day comes to an end
Another bunch I've gathered, I now can send,
But, to give each one an early start
I send these roses from within my heart . . .

Brian Ducker

TO SNIP OR NOT TO SNIP?

What a pleasant time of year
When nature tells us spring is here,
Daffs are blooming
Birds are swooning
Frogs are spawning
Leaves adorning.
The trouble is it gets him going
Amorous conduct he starts showing,
A dog so placid, I tell no lie
I would even say he's shy.
But when his hormones start to rise
Too much contact is unwise.
You see, Bensy gets a bit confused
Hence your leg becomes abused,
Being a lad of seven stone
This behaviour I can't condone,
Cushions conquested
Teddies molested
Friends are harassed
I'm embarrassed,
I warn him loudly with the *snip*!
Onto his back he does flip,
Another chance from me he gets
Avoiding a visit to the vets,
Well, with legs akimbo he's so cute,
Not the usual sex-crazed brute,
So, his tiresome danglies he will keep
I hate to see a big dog weep,
I'm still hoping
He'll stop groping
He's now calmer
What a charmer.

Pauline Jones

THE AWAKENING

Awakening of emotions,
New life and rebirth,
Like gentle rays of sunshine
Warming frozen earth.

The changing of the seasons
And the joy they bring,
Filling hearts with boundless love,
The first touch of spring.

Heavily scented mornings,
Dew drop laden grass,
Passions build like fires within
That nothing can surpass.

Dreamy azure heavens,
With little sign of cloud,
Small creatures gambol playfully,
Tall trees stand so proud.

Fulfilment of all senses,
Knowing life is free,
The mind and body joined as one
For all eternity.

Forget the chill of winter,
Let all love abound
Throughout the changing seasons,
To last the whole year round.

Anne Frances Wilson

GHOST OF A LOVER

As I view the sinking Tuscan sun
And watch the fireflies glow
I sense that you are near,
I sip my wine and contemplate,
Who were *you*? Who was I?

I love this land of the Etruscans
Beauty lives here, in colour and sunlight,
Art and music, the food of life,
Castles, hilltop towns, history,
I am free here, yet I am your prisoner.

Why do you torment and taunt me?
You reach out and call me back.
Your power is infinite
I obey and return to you
When spring is in the air.

Must I forever ponder your hidden secrets?
And yet I *know* you, from another time
Your dark eyes flashing full of fire
Your smile, I know so well,
We were lovers, you and I.

In some secret bower or poppy field,
As the sun hung, glimmering in the sky
And the warm breeze caressed us,
We lingered under the dark blue velvet sky,
And night became our friend.

My heart rejoices, my soul is yours,
Calm your troubled spirit,
Be patient a little longer
Soon I'll be with you
By the sapphire lake of eternity.

Edith Sanders

SPRING IS IN THE AIR

First sun in April
An astounding day
All green and leafy
Makes me want to play

Learning to love again
Seems like the very first
Your touch like soft rain
On me the flower; thrust -
Our lips each other tendering
Asking - is this real?

Yvonne S Wirtz

SPEAK OF A BLUE MOON

So many ways to speak.
Actions loud, in sleep.
Land upon land and from beak.
Bland to brand new
With most I haven't a clue.
Musical melody sources a tear,
While I sign a tune to him that can feel
The vibrations that could never satisfy the multitude.
Could it be magic? Or should I pray to St Jude?
For a practised denomination, to break through
The essence of the purest of its art.
And a pure love rekindled in a spark.
Under a moon of blue
I'm almost afraid to speak.
There is no need to speak.
I know it's you.

Kenneth Leddy

SPRING IS IN THE AIR

A crisp golden morning,
Dew upon the grass green.
Flowers slowly budding,
A bird's answer to a dream.

The park that is slowly awakening,
Lovers strolling hand in hand.
In the distance wedding bells chiming,
Carnival troupers dance to a band.

Lambs dance in the fields,
Baby birds try and fly from the nest.
Animals refreshed from hibernation,
Awaken from a long winter's rest.

A P Plant

THE SEASON OF GOODBYES

The blossom was appearing, on trees both old and young.
It was the season of beginnings, of new life just begun.
It was not the season of goodbyes, that's autumn time I'd say,
And yet we had to bid farewell, forever and a day.
Life had not been dreary, there wasn't any row,
But someone took his love away and that is how
It came to pass, that I was left alone.
My mind was blank, feeling numb and heart was like a stone.
Never had I know such love that filled me full and full.
Such blessings of a sweet romance I hadn't known at all,
Until I met this dear, dear friend . . . was his name,
And in my prayers both night and day I plead, return again.

Sara Jayne Rettie

WHAT IS IT?

Today I've had that feeling,
My nostrils twitching can smell it too.
It's nothing I've seen, like the bulbs pushing through.
It's nothing I've heard like the bold cuckoo.
It's the hairs on the back of my neck standing up.
It's my head lifting up to the sky.
It's my heart that is dancing and wanting to sing,
Don't you know it? Can't you feel it?
Aren't you certain?
It's spring,
            It's spring,
                        It's spring.

A' O' E'

WHITE BLOSSOM

Winter has lessened its grip on the land
Chased by spring's white blossom of hope.
While the sun dances late to a band
And the cold nights hang by a rope.

Lambs gambol in fields of green grass
While birds nest in leafy trees.
Bedding plants are bought with hard brass
And gardens now are buzzing with bees.

Barbecues are out now and burning
Often curtailed by storms of rain
While the spring of life keeps turning
Enjoyed by us all in the main.

Denise Bonham

THE AWAKENING

Spring, O spring, what words can be said?
As you shake the snowdrops loose from your head,
You blink the winter out of your eyes,
And stretch out your beauty under pristine blue skies.

Hark! The breeze rustles through woodland and field,
Carrying your perfume on invisible heels,
Fresh and heady from the new virgin queen,
It enfolds around magic and polishes dreams.

Go; seek out Woodawose, young Jack in the Green,
Beguile him with beauty, and touches serene,
Entice him from the woodlands - away to the hills,
May he chase to caress you and grasp at your frills.

Let your coupling be slow, yet intense with desire,
May it spread through the land, as a warm burning fire,
Giving birth to the hedgerows, the spinney, the copse,
Touching rivers, ponds and ditches, with emerald green locks.

Your birth pangs are wonder, unfolding with life,
Enchanted and vibrant, enveloped in light,
May your protégé grow, giving thanks for their birth,
To their emerald green mother, who gave them their birth.

John C Sutton

SPRING

S is for the *season* which we all can see.
P is for the *popping* of buds on the tree.
R is for the *rivers* rolling by in a rush.
I is for an *inkling* of flowers on the bush.
N is for the *new* life that regularly appears.
G is for the *great* feelings it heralds every year.

Helen Steel

SPRING 'TIME OUT'

The pansies are in bloom
in the pots on the balcony
their sunny faces open to the sun.
Hyacinths protrude seductively
awaiting the warm caress
that will release their fragrance.

You have left the door ajar
and the spring breeze sneaks in
through dusty lace
undressing my winter cares
chilling bare skin
deliciously.

Magnolia light dances
transforming your sleeping face
softening well known contours.
The breeze wafts smells of you
in my direction.
I snuggle closer.

I trace your eyebrow
with a finger tip
The moment is mine to treasure -
the conductor holding the orchestra
before the performance.

I shall wake you now
and with a stolen kiss
create a bottled memory.
You will take the day off
winter goals behind you
and the summer yet to come . . .

Chrissy Smith

DIVINE SATISFACTION

My self-esteem is soaring high,
This time of year's the reason why.
My mind's obsessed with sensual intentions,
My body combines and wants to venture.
Let me arouse your inner passion,
Take off those clothes, you need no fashion.
Your body scent spurs my fascination,
I can't hold back, I need satisfaction,
Let me explore your masculine charms,
Lay back, relax, be calm.
Enter into fantasy land,
Come hold on tight and take my hand.
This is the place to let yourself go,
Stretch out your body down to your toes.
Right now you're in paradise,
Fleshy shapes together, it will be alright.
Raunchily our bodies touch,
These emotions I lust.
Our bodily appetites' taking over,
Intimacy arising, we're getting closer.
Erotically we move and sway,
Divine satisfaction I'd say.

Karla Hutchins

GLACIER GARDEN

Oh! Happy Greenland, why are you so blue,
When my heart is true to be with you?
I pray and lull to temporary sleep
Your soul and mine to keep.
We float amongst the spell of natural beauty,
Your atmospheric song, a lullaby of the flautist winds.

My life, I give to you; my gain,
The prize reflected in my mystic eyes,
Your wondrous eternal smile to change my all.
Enveloping silence mists, cover your pale complexion.
Your firelight eyes melt as waters ice.
Parting with soothing teardrops, you fade to disappear.
Reach and stretch your hands to mine,
So that we may walk, together through time.

Anthony Keyes

THE SPRING

Most of us dislike the winter,
Days of darkness, curtains drawn,
Suet pudding, stew and dumplings,
People looking all forlorn.

Then we see the dainty snowdrop
Flowering on the compost heap,
Winter jasmine, orange berries,
Mother Nature's not asleep.

Spring is just around the corner,
Winter's on its weary way.
Crocus, daffodil and tulip,
Colours brighten up our day.

Birds are nesting in the hedgerow,
Buds are bursting on the tree.
Words cannot describe the beauty
Given us each day to see.

Very soon it will be Easter,
Chocolate eggs and Simnel cake,
Lilies in the church on Sunday
Give us cause to celebrate.

Phyllis M Iden

TRANSITION

Silently it drops to the ground,
and very quickly it covers the mounds.
I look around and what do I see,
a blanket of white all around like a sea.
I look again, the sun comes out,
the blanket is gone, it's green all about.
The snow that was there us gone from us now.
A beautiful spring day is shining for us, *wow*.

Marion Lee

SPRINGTIME LOVE

It's springtime once again
And I'm looking for romance
I get this feeling every spring
So I'm taking one more chance,
Last year I found a boyfriend
I thought he was the one
But by the time the season passed
My springtime was no longer fun
We used to play around in fields
And cuddle in the hay
Telling how much we loved each other
It wasn't true I'm sorry to say
As he held my hand and kissed me
The air seemed full of spring
Until one day he walked out of my life
So now I am searching again

Pamela Hole

LEO

Leo lion strut your stuff
for it is just not enough
centre of attention you must be
no such thing as equality

When one does stroke your fur
and you oh so gently purr
a strong leader you can be
full of sexuality

Centre stage, party out
no time for any self doubt
like a magnificent bear you roar
but only on the surface soar

As you stroke your long mane
looking for the one to tame
search no more for I am here
this much is evidently clear

Leo is full of confidence
seeking limelight and credence
love to hear some flattery
though only with sincerity

Leo a tom cat for sure
and in your den you may lure
pretty young kittens to see you through
for subtlety just ain't you!

Gena K Crawford

'NOW' - SPRING IS IN THE AIR

If I don't write this now
I probably never will.

Who's to say?

I've had a glass or two of
wine

And it frees me to express
what otherwise would go

Unsaid.

Is that unwise or merely a pity?

So many times I've seen a
ray of hope

A flame to warm myself by

Only to watch it flicker or even
die should I look too closely.

Now is the time to
explore or expel.

Now is the time of plain
truths and open hearts.

Or what is the point?

Either we have courage
or we do not.

Then all is little but a game.

If you have feelings
then express them.

If you have need of me
then voice it.

Either by sound or
more worthily

A single kiss.

If a previous experience has
made you afraid

Then this I cannot change.

I can only show you
A different ending.

June Elliott

SPRING FEAST

As dew lays on sodden ground
Pink cherry blossom hangs all around
Small buttercups grow here and there
A gentle breeze blows through her hair.

Her picnic basket lies on the grass
And she prepares her meal at last
A meal that's worthy of a king
She starts to eat, birds start to sing.

Juicy tomatoes, big and round
A large pork pie that weighs a pound
Delicious sandwiches made with ham
And current buns coated with jam.

Near where she sits a young lamb leaps
And a spotted snake slowly creeps
And now the sun shines in the spring
Who knows what joy its new life will bring.

Joanne Harrington (13)

NEW SPRING

She was the epitome of spring.
All the charm of the birds
All the beauty of the flowers,
Enveloped into one creature.
She would capture my gaze
And then force me to smile,
It was true I didn't know her.
But she held me prisoner
To all her whims and whyfores
If only one day I could speak to her

She must think me a fool
For I never utter a word to her,
But surely it is infinitely
Better to be thought a fool,
Than to speak and remove all doubt.
Yet these symptoms of love
They grow so strong when she's near,
And when I see her all else fails
My mind will not function
And I wish for the floor to give way.

Michael D Watson

WILL YOU MARRY ME?

Peter Robinson was his name
I proposed to him all the same.
Mum was shocked when she was told
Said I shouldn't have been so bold.
I thought I was in seventh heaven
Peter was six and I was seven.

P M Low

PARIS IN THE SPRING

I fell in love with Paris,
When spring was in the air.
The glistening white *Montmatre*
Is where I left my care,
And 'Oh!' The Eiffel Tower
Beside the sparkling *Seine*.
I fell in love with Paris,
I shall return again.
The *Notre Dame* cathedral
The lovers on the *Left Bank*.
The shops and all the people,
The Metro under city 'Clank'.
I fell in love with Paris,
When Spring was in the air.
You'll know just what I mean,
If you ever visit there.

June V Johnson

SO GREAT THE LOVE

So great the love I feel for him
Yet he knows not even my name
The burning passion that lies in the depths of my heart
It consumes my very soul
Gladly I would give up one thousand of my days alone
For one beautiful day in his sweet presence.

Andrea Murdock

LOVE IN THE SPRING

When spring comes around
Young lovers are found
In parks and in towns
Their love knows no bounds
As they cling together
Whatever the weather.

Like frisky young lambs
They frolic and play
And sounds of their laughter
Are heard all the day.

They kiss and they cuddle
Their arms entwined
In a world of their own
To the rest of us blind.

So make haste young lovers
Take love while you may
We wish you much happiness
All of your days.

P Southwell

TREASURES OF SPRING

The days of spring are filled with gold.
Soon just a memory is winter's cold.
The forsythia bush with stars bright
Heralds the spring with a golden light.
The daffodils too in the borders near
Wear a gold halo now spring is here.

But deep in the shade of the woodland bower
Here shall we find the fairest flower.
With a delicate grace and perfume slight
A golden heart and a fringe of light.
This *princess of spring* sits quietly by
Near where the wren and the blackbird fly.
A *princess*, you ask, or maybe she's *queen?*
Oh! Didn't I tell you? The *primrose* I mean.

Marion Snow

SPRING BREAK BY THE COAST

Sex in Sussex
on a sofa.
Rented cottage,
lousy weather.
Couldn't even see the pier.
Feeling randy,
now spring's here.

Sex in Sussex,
nice three-seater.
Faded curtains,
gas by meter.
Book the same place every year.
Somewhere sandy
fairly near.

Sex in Sussex
on stretch covers.
Perfect spot for nature lovers.
Take home pizza,
local beer,
very handy
full of cheer.

Malcolm Brown

THIS ENCHANTED LADY

This enchanted lady has entered my life
For she is a rose among roses
She has brought a ray of light into my dark world
This darkness is beyond words and meaning

For her love of life is my reward
Her charm and beauty there is no equal
The music of the night is ours
For as we danced upon the floor
We were poetry in motion

As our bodies embraced
Such tenderness I have never known
We see no-one upon the floor
Only the two of us together
She dances like a falling leaf
Drifting in the wind so pure and gently

As we danced upon air
We hear no music only the music of our hearts
Two hearts beating as one
If only the night could last for eternity
This all that I ask
If only this enchanted lady
Was mine to have and hold forever

As we danced the last dance
The music of the night fades away
Must this night of nights end
For she is my very life and love
No greater dream do I have
Oh this enchanted lady

Penny Lover

SPRING IS IN THE AIR

Spring makes me think of bluebells
Growing in the woods in May
Like a blue carpet spread out
So lovely among the trees

But it also reminds me
Of my courting days when young
Of lying together there
With the scent of bluebells
Filling the air around us

The sound of the river nearby
Babbling along in the sun
Completing this spring picture
Remembered from long ago

Now spring is so different
The bluebells are still there
And I walk among them
But now I'm not with my lover

The sun still shines down on us
The water still shimmers there
But now you are not with me
My grandson is walking here.

Margaret C Rae

SPRINGTIME AT CILGERRIN

Let's away to Cilgerrin Castle,
A magical place to be,
When ancient turf springs once more into life,
And shrub and branch dance with glee.

See there a maid and companion,
Strolling 'neath ramparts in bud,
She dreams of gentle loving,
While his mind's full of battles and blood.

For he's slain ten thousand dragons
In the winter fields of foe,
And cannot feel spring's warm caress
With a heart hard-packed in snow.

Spring's blanket stretches before them,
'Daisies - oh daisies!' she cries,
And draws him into the midst of them,
'I'll make you a crown' he replies.

Her words ride on arrows from Cupid,
And each one dispatched finds its place,
There tingles, explodes and bursts into song,
Though not a note is displayed on his face.

Cross-legged he sits, busy working,
By his side she does not stir,
As hands that spilt blood for a nation,
Create beauty - just for her.

So we'll leave our long shackled hero,
Oblivious to what has begun,
In the magical shade of Cilgerrin,
Threading daisies, one by one.

Paula Walke

RAINBOW GOLD

How welcome April's pleasures.
Show to the birds and bees
And budding trees unfold
for a new beginning tell us
For all mankind plan bold
New hopes to dreams
Like blossoms flourish
Young love for romance schemes
For old love fulfilment dreams
And simple pleasures
More precious than gold
Like the solitary baby silver
Birch tree, blushing happily
In the rainbow glow.

Phyllis Moseley Clayton

NON STARTER

Sitting alone,
awaiting my friend.
Ten more minutes I'll wait,
I think this is a trend.

Still sitting alone,
my friend she is great.
Blonde and attractive,
but also very late.

Alone still I sit,
Yes still I hear you cry.
If she turns up now,
I'll stand up and say goodbye

Robert Collins

MORNING WALK
(For Dominique)

Into the morning calm I step
Fresh, from the depth of relaxed sleep.
As yet no traffic noise to hide
The songs of birds, from every side.

As past the church with bells yet still
I ease my pace down the long hill
From rooftops, eaves and dew-soaked trees,
The birdsong swells, my life to please.

Past the wood so full of sound
Sweet birdsong fills the air around.
Across the stream, so fresh so clear
As nature sheds a joyful tear.

Into the valley, as the mist
As if by order slowly lifts
Revealing the glory to be seen
Nature's pastures, new life green.

Then sudden warmth, sun's fresh ray
Sets aglow the wakening day.

Back up the hill the church bells ring
In harmony the birds all sing.
Each part of God's great symphony
This story they are telling me.

Joy of joy - now with us sing
Winter is past, *come welcome spring!*

ANB

LOVE IS . . .

Love is . . . when you care for someone,
Love isn't when you're shy,
To find it hard to let the other know,
When you wish to cry.

Love is . . . holding on to someone,
Feeling sad when they are sad,
Love is . . . loving the other one,
Even when they're mad.

Love is . . . coping with each problem,
Sharing as you go,
Love is . . . growing closer to them,
Letting feelings show.

Love is . . . having warm embraces,
Not caring who can see,
Love is . . . focusing alone on you,
And you alone on me.

Love is . . . cheering someone up,
Especially when they're down,
Love is . . . finding ways to make them smile,
To wipe away their frown.

And don't forget that when you've argued,
it's really really fun,
To make up with that special person,
'Cos love is . . . *when you're one!*

Maria Cracknell

POPPIES

Today they're wearing *lived-in* hats
of panama and straw - so summer's come!
They both wore woollen ones before.
He walks behind her with a stick.
She's still quite nimble - he's not so quick.

Always measured space between them
joined by an unseen strand
linked together by living
no need to talk or hold his hand.
Sprightly minds, they smile and chat
with gardeners along the way
swapping yarns of gardens gone
before they gently travel on.

In the springtimc of their walking days
she'd ask and softly sigh
'Is this summer dear?'
And smiling he'd reply
'Not until the poppies bloom.'
But a lifetime spent together
brings winter all too soon
and the sad sweet sound of a robin.

Betty Norris

SPRINGTIME

The trees have been standing
gaunt and bare, forever, or so it seems
but if you look closely, you will see
browns turning into greens

Leaves and blossom will soon abound
for this is the season of spring
and snowdrops and violets cover the ground
and birds begin to sing

We wonder who will be the first to see
the newly-born lambs as they play
or see the first swallow or hear
the first cuckoo call his weary roundelay

And before we can see all the beauties of spring
it will change into long lazy days
so enjoy it all before it is gone
melted into summer's warm haze.

Jenny Brownjohn

STEPHEN

Why do I love you?
On my days of
Greasy hair
Black, shadowed eyes
And clothes fit for Oxfam,
You still believe
I'm a beautiful, towered maiden.
When I need someone to turn to
You are there for tears
To moisten the shoulders
Of your warm, comfortable shirts.
We can argue like alley cats
But never care who wins.
We'll share a lifetime of emotion
Watch people come and go
And always be together
Even when apart.
Because you're who you are
I no longer hold my heart.

Carol Fearnall

SPRINGTIME

Welcome signs of brighter days to come
Are the warming rays of the morning sun
Spring arriving, sights to greet
Are new lambs in fields, as in pleasure bleat
A new beginning to see is very clear
As leaves on trees slowly appear
March winds have cleared the winter air
As April showers the ground prepares
Apple blossom, white and pure shows its face
A contrast to the glow of cherry blossom grace
Stormy weather leaves its mark being naughty
As it blows the blossom to the ground like confetti
The warmth of the sun urges bulbs to come hither
But in the cold of night do they shiver
As Jack Frost likes to takc his time to depart
He's cold and frosty, has no heart
Lawns have grown and now need cutting
Short grass is better when golfers are putting
The children now play their outdoor games
Excited and energetic, being no longer tamed
When May arrives everywhere is full of life
For days are longer and we have more light
As days are now getting warmer for all
The elderly too hear the outside call
Don their coats and venture for a stroll again
It makes a change from winds and rain
Sport is again enjoyed outside by all
And most are played with bats and balls
Everyone is pleased now that spring has returned
And feel it is doing them - a very good turn.

M J Morris

TWO LOVERS

Two lovers stood looking not a word was said,
Alone in their sorrow, a tear instead.
What sorrow, what grief, oh how their hearts ache,
They know what's to be done, their hearts will break.
Together, a single smile says they must part,
Alone again, each one a new life to start.
Each hand clasped tightly must slowly unfold,
A lingering look, their eyes meet, a story untold.
A last kiss, a tender kiss on a tear-stained cheek,
But only these two know wherever they seek.
The love they had for that short while,
Will keep in their hearts to hold in a smile.
Two lovers look back as the years go by,
A sad smile on their face a tear in their eye.
To part was the decision made that night,
But only time will tell if the answer was right.

Maralyn Major

THE WEEPING WILLOW

You really have a sad life
Your head is always down
Your long arms are left dangling
Your face is just a frown

At night your position is just the same
As if it were the day
You move when the wind helps you to
Another angle, another way

At night when couples sit under your arms
You shelter them from the world outside
So why are you always *weeping willow?*
Stand up tall with grace and pride.

Donna Simpson

ETERNAL EMBRACE

A transfixed trance,
  That was meaningful and deep,
Pierced through to his soul,
  To discover secrets
That I could keep,
  Tears in my eyes,
Like a bore at high tide,
  Dry lips caressed each others,
As the love that was flowing
  We did not want to hide,
Our hearts
  Were beating in unison,
At the sound of double base,
  I could observe every emotion,
By each crease,
  In his smooth skinned face,
His arms were locked around me,
  Like the binding of eternal love,
This is one emotion,
  One could never be tiresome of.

Della Clark

SPRING

Spring, spring is everywhere,
hear the laughter in the trees.
Flowers are beginning to bud,
giving pollen to the bees.

Dandelions reflect the sun,
watery and bright.
Trees are growing their petals,
Cherry pink and apple blossom white.

Everywhere people are gardening,
making their lawns look their best.
Birds come down from the sky,
gathering cuttings for their nest.

Spring, spring is everywhere,
more than a fair share of rainbows,
giving people renewed optimism
while helping to find their pot of gold.

Andrew Downs

EXPRESSING LOVE

Expressing love and how we feel.
From deep within our hearts.
It is the biggest gift of all.
It has a special art.

Some people write their words in songs.
Some people have to sing it.
Some people do it with a gift.
A poem is best when in it.

Attractions draw you to someone.
Arousing interest you go on.
To know this person that stirs your soul.
Leaves you feeling there's an empty hole.

Who would have thought that love could be
So powerful in your soul.
Intensity so deep for thee.
The feelings grow and grow.

A tender kiss a hug for more.
Your bodies meet as one.
Entwining souls love unfolds.
That art with a special one.

Delline Docherty

SUNRISE

The black night shrinks
          into its banished place,
Lies, skulking,
          waiting for another day to end.
The crimson disc rises
          over the dark bleak tops,
Showering its warm welcome
          on its friends.

Dewdrops lie in a bouquet of flowing mist
Enveloping fresh emerald grasses.
Evaporates, spirals silently upwards,
Slowly passes . . . into the awakening sky.
Bells of dawning call.
Day awakens in golden glory.
The whistles of a thousand birds
Promise the start of another story.

Athol Cowen

WELCOME, ANOTHER SPRING!

Plants flaunt their joy in bold
Gestures and arabesques
Of green and gold -
New life's exuberance
Bursts from damp mould.
Predating man or god
Orchid and rose
Made all earth beautiful
Where no foot trod.
Coal-ferns thrust a pose
Up in delight,
And there was light.

Bevil Grenville

SPRING IS IN THE AIR

Spring is in the air
Flowers are blooming everywhere.
Everything is starting to grow
And in all of us it is starting to show.

Some days are full of sunshine
And everything looks so fine.
And other days are filled with rain
But that is the wonderful thing about spring no day is the same.

Spring is in the air
So beware,
You might start to feel strange,
As you watch everything change.

Like a snake we seem to shed an old skin
And on new journeys we begin.
Life is starting like new,
There are changes we are all going through.

Spring is in the air
So prepare,
For everyone is acting a little oddly
But it is just their spirits being set free.

Everything has turned green
And we are all walking around in a dream.
The world is taking on a new life
And nothing feels quite right.

Katharine Hall

YESTERDAY

Yesterday was so nice, up on the moors
just you and me alone together,
with no-one else within miles of us,
except the sheep and baby lambs.

we found a secluded place behind some rocks,
sitting down,
we looked at the beautiful, surrounding countryside
and then we made love in the sun.

on the way back down the hill, we stopped,
as a baby lamb slowly came over to us,
then it ran back to its mother
and together they ran away.

hand in hand
we walked slowly back to your car,
then we had to go back home
as you had to go to work.

the morning had been so nice
one of the best times yet,
the sun was shining
from the moment we were together,
and stayed like it for most of the day.

if only the world had stopped
when we were locked together,
it would have been so beautiful
up on that hill,
just you and me together.

Linda Casey

KISSING IN THE RAIN

Thick clouds tumbling across the sky,
Turn darker shades before they cry.
And then it really begins to pour.
What were you doing a moment before?
Shelter under the clouds above,
Washing out the colours of love.
Holding hands, soaked to the skin,
A happy feeling deep from within.
Closer still then sweet embrace,
I wipe the wet hair from your face.
Secrets softly begin to unfold,
A love better than a pot of gold.
Hoping it would all come to this,
A passionate end of the rainbow kiss.

Kevin J Foulger

A LADYBIRD

I lay down in the sun
And found myself being picked
Up by something for fun.
This was soft and warm
I knew it would not harm
And a warm feeling swept over me.
I was picked up by a child
So meek and mild
And they put me down with
A gentle touch,
And it didn't hurt me much.
I guess you have guessed
I am a ladybird!

Sallie Sarjant-Tugwell

COWSLIPS

Spring has come, the sap is rising
Moss is growing, looking for moisture.
Jade green, olive brown, deep emerald
The first flowers of the year begin to shoot.

A nearby field is where we go
To gather up a treasure trove
A steep hill is what we must find
And climb and climb and climb.

Look there they are like gems of topaz
Glinting in the sunshine
The brimstone among flowers
The sweetest smell, like honey, drifts towards me,
The beauty; the carpet of gold
It's as though we've had a shower of yellow rain
Which in turn has filled the field full of yellow ochre

I pick one after another, till,
The bunch is too large to hold.

The wind howls. It's so cold.
A cry carried towards me
I must go
I love spring and the cowslips
That vivid colour - that wondrous smell
A once a year chance of a lifetime.

Linnet-Joy Allison

TOUCH MY HEART

Strong hands caress my face
Then worn fingers stroke my neck,
Your hot breath kisses my ear
As I recline in this sweltering reality.

As sounds drift through this oppressive heat
I feel your touch transporting me,
To a distant time and different life
Where you and I once lived.

Outside, revellers start to dwindle
We are alone in the darkness of night,
And as your hands smooth my hair
Your eyes call me into your heart.

As you are whispering into my ear,
I lift my head to kiss you,
We are alone and all consumed
By blinding emotions that bind us.

Alone in this silent white room
Uttering incomprehensible sounds,
We understand only these touches
And embark on this life's great adventure.

Later, as you awake beside me
And our bodies still are cooling,
I look into your eyes and see
Them telling me that you love me.

C Beardmore

WATCHING

Watching the time go by
Waiting for the door to knock
Lying on my bed and thinking of your love
Always wondering if it's true, but
remembering that I love you.
Smiling at the memories I have which
you gave me on those timeless nights.
Why does love feel this way?
Wanting and needing your tender touch
imagining your lips gently teasing mine.
Closing my eyes and I feel you holding me
and awakening my inner feelings,
oh the passion and the fire between us
is building greater and greater,
when heaven seems so close.
I awake alone remembering my dream,
I sit a little dazed, scan the room
for some hope of a sense of reality,
when on my pillow I find a single red rose
with the words 'I love you.'
So maybe it wasn't a dream but there again
life is just an exciting dream.
Maybe I'll relax, lie back and begin my dream again.

Nadia Dawn Camila

SAYING GOODBYE

Tears in your eyes
Well, we've said our goodbyes
And I wish I could dry
Your tears.

You're growing up
And will conquer your fears
As experience comes
With the added years

I love you my son
But I must let you go
Holding on too long
Will not help you grow
In every sense of the word

Still, you'll soon be back
If that is God's will
More assured and with clear eyes
All the same I wish still
That I'd had more time
To help cope with your fears.

Well, that's life my son
That is how it begun
And also how it will end
See you soon I hope
Meanwhile we must cope
With a smile on our face
For 'Hello.'

Johanna van Gorkom

GUENDALYN (LAND OF THE RISING SUN)

Soft thin sunrise eyes
smile white petal rose dune fragrance
arousing bedridden bones
slumbering deep darkness.

The hinne-ni dew doused flower fists
draw warm wet breath
unfurling imbibed synchronous lip raiment
Revealing peeling full moon nectar
towards an insouciant heaven
Puckering purl ground, bristle pool,
atmospheric cocktail kisses
Bonding tongue twined lovers
intimately embracing cupidity.

He, She, kiss-whisper
'Sleeping spirit,
I missed you last night,
let us rejoice awakening
and throw whittled shadow gist images, rattling,
they accompany no more.'

Light fast shoots past,
rushing, revolving,
thrusting gravity animated axis
swirling.

Dark light, light dark.
She kisses him. He kisses her.
They make ageing time,
struggling survival
to brittle croak crooning crone;
Zimmer-frame supported night.

Away she wisps, farewell,
stroking sleep tight,
lights out, and tucked in.

Under the dusk blanket cat eyed cocoon
he curls inwards
reaching lengthening shadows
in the fetal position
tearfully sprouting her departure
longing tomorrow's return.

Lawrance-Marc Richards

WHEN SPRING IS IN THE AIR

When spring is in the air
Catkins swing in the breeze,
Primroses are in bloom,
And buds burst forth on trees.
In the fields the rabbits run,
Young cows and horses feed,
Lambs cry for their mothers
Some food is all they need.

When spring is in the air
Frogs croak throughout the night,
Spawn appears on the pond,
Soon tadpoles are in sight.
The blackbird builds her nest
From twigs and moss and leaves,
He does not help at all
But sings from tops of trees.

When spring is in the air
The grass begins to grow,
Lawnmowers make a noise
When people start to mow.
The garden needs a trim,
The house is cleaned up too,
Wedding bells are ringing
New clothes for me and you.

Muriel R Wrigley

THE LOVE SEASON

Winter's gone at long last,
Gone cold nights, and monkeys brassed.
The sun's returned with amber tone,
Romance now wakes, from love's seed sown.

Young loves will walk hand in hand,
Down country lane, 'long seashore's sand.
Their eyes will meet, their lips will kiss,
Their moment shared, their covert bliss.

On window sill bird chorus sings,
Now couples pledged will seek rings.
They scheme, they plan a life together,
With inner passion, and outer tether.

The winter shells cracked open wide,
Now pearls of love are free to ride.
As days get long, night losses grip
There's liquid love for all to sip.

Nicholas Short

ALL COLOURS OF THE RAINBOW

On a clear day we remember, down at the coast
Long hot sultry summer, simmering barbecue roast
Then quick as a flash, dark clouds over the terrain
Loud thunder and lightning and down poured the rain

So heavy was the rain, almost like a monsoon
The heavens had opened up, torrential rain that soon
Changed to the extreme and to our delight
Suddenly the rain stopped and the sky turned bright
High in the sky, a massive arc of light
All the colours of the rainbow, an unforgettable sight.

Rita Humphrey

PLEASE BE SPRING

A frosty path, a frosty tree
Winter has got its grip of me
Water frozen white and hard
One flower standing stiff as a card
Cold fingers begin to sing
Hurry oh hurry! Please be spring
Darkness with fog appears
A hazy moon through the mist leers
While frost in patterns on the grass
Leaves crusted together in a mass
Hurry, oh hurry! Please be spring
On bright days we get warmth from the sun
But the cold comes back as soon as it's gone
You slip and slide risking bones
That's why people stay in their homes
As winter passes, I'll say one thing
Hurry, oh hurry! Please be spring.

Harry Fox

SPRING IS SPRUNG

Late in coming season's thirst
Offers treasure's flowers first
Requited garland's clustered face
Many coloured petals traced

Soils moist yet touched and found
Shows a seed's enabled mound
While Victoria's modest green
Ages sapling's sheltered dream.

David A Bennett

WHERE IS LOVE?

Where is this love, this rhapsody
Of which the poets sing
This grand awakening of the heart
This glorious burgeoning?

Where is this thing that they call love
Why does it pass me by
Why, Cupid, do you stay your dart
And never let it fly?

Why have I never know its bliss
Or yet its bitter pain
Why do I wander far and wide
And lonely still remain?

Seeking within somebody's eye
A sudden radiant gleam
A look of wonder and surprise
Must it remain a dream?

Must it forever be my quest
To search, and never find
Why, fates, will you not once relent
And always be unkind?

My heart must ever silent be
A melody unplayed
And I must wander through the years
Alone, forlorn, afraid.

Sybil Sibthorpe

IMAGES IN SPRING

I saw you standing there, but
words refused to come.
The atmosphere electrified! Oh fool
to be struck dumb!
Unexpectedly the two of us
compelled to hesitate and look
into the soul of the other
and as sometimes a new book
will hold our attention
to the very end,
so this spirit of spring enfolded us -
and I recognised a friend!

See how clouds drift high and
billowing in the air -
the softness and the rosy hue of one
reflected in the other there.
So may any small particle of
tenderness that is mine
be transmitted my love and
in some distant time
you will be glad, as I,
that we exchanged the image
of the spring, and
did not pass by.

We paused just to watch the seasons ebb and flow -
entwined our fingers . . . never to let go!

Peggy Briston

SPRING PROMISE

The sumach's parasol parades
Its half-formed canopy above spring's early flowers
I have until the May light fades
To build the shed it says will take two hours

Along the ivy's tendrils cling
The last drops of the early morning rain
My hammer's head, with awesome ring,
Departs the shaft and wrecks the virgin pane

The missel-thrush picks up a worm
And soars to perch upon the dying oak
The lilac's swollen buds are firm
Tomorrow's tree will wear its purple cloak

The sweat upon my brow owes nought
To sunbeams simpering through the rowan tree
The holes in panel A which ought
Just do not match the dowels in panel B

A starling squabble over bread
Lets in marauding sparrows who then flee
To where their young are safely fed
Leaving their droppings over panel C

The copper-burnished berberis
Is fired to brilliance by the midday sun
I don't know where my spanner is
The glue on panel D's begun to run

The daffodil's last petals flake
An evening breeze sends, kite-like, overhead
The plan which promised it would take
Two hours to build this sodding, sodding shed.

Tom Owen

WINTER PASSION

What are people doing
    With their houses all aglow?
What do people think
    When their gardens fill with snow?
Orange-haze haloed
    In the greying sky
Lamps are lit.
Perhaps they dream of summer
Foreign customs, foreign climes?
When houses are inviting
Homes find friends and love.
    Rose-hip,
    Rose lips,
    Berries appassionata.

Irene Patricia Kelly

LOVE SONG

If you love me as I love you
you'll know just how I feel
our vows were ever binding
our dreams are oh so real.

Our thirteen years of marriage
have brought us closer still
and for every year that passes
I know it always will.

Sometimes I think of losing you
and the tears just start to flow
so please please always stay with me
and say you'll never go.

Dorothy Johnstone

BY SMILING BEAMS

The warming sun which lay so long
enshrined in winter's chill
begins to rise with life renewed.

By sunny rays love's cheeks
to blossom begin to turn
colouring to rosy red, the winter's pale.

The warming sun transforming
all within her gaze,
love's petals opening
by her touch of warmth.

By smiling beams she warms
the heart of love,
winter's coolness dispersing
with her sunshine smiles.

The warming sun the gift of love
has stirred -
two lovers entwine beneath
her pleasing glance.

Gary Shields

HAPPY DAY

Let this be a happy day
All the while and all the way
With all the happy memories
That passing years have brought.

When blooms are scarce
And flowers are rare
Spring brings the light
To guide us on our way.

The happy days of long ago
Always seem the best of all
But time cannot be halted
With what this day may leave.

Time be good and life be kind
We know so much, yet have not understood
The simple truth of the bygone days
But memory opens the door on a happy day like this.

Heather Aspinall

YOU MUST BE KIDDING!

Spring?
Yes, it's spring!
With frost striding across gardens,
scything the tender new growth.

Spring?
Yes, it's spring!
With wind roaring through trees,
shredding the soft new leaves.

Spring?
Yes, it's spring!
With rain lashing on blossom,
drenching the bright new flowers.

Spring?
Yes, it's spring!
With cold creeping into nests,
chilling the tiny new birds.

Spring?
Yes, it's spring!
With love huddling on back seats,
necking in thermals and socks.

Anne Mansell

MAKING LOVE

Looking.
Smiling.
Touching.
Embrace.
Warm tender kisses planted on face.
Kissing,
Harder,
Tongues inside.
Pressing together our bodies collide.
Holding,
Gripping.
I look in your eyes,
Our bodies are merging and so are our minds.
Pressing.
Undressing.
Take you I must,
Our minds taken over with primeval lust.
Moaning,
Grunting,
Clenching of teeth.
The rhythm excels to its final release.
Looking,
Smiling,
Touching,
Embrace.
Warm tender kisses planted on face.

C D Hammond

FAREWELL POEM

When I see you again
Summer will be passing,
Spring a vague memory.
Days will have worn our thoughts
Into memories.
Winter will be closer
By three months, and you
A little older.

The flowers in the fields
Will be ageing then,
And the woods will be full
Of summer's creations.
Lovers will be found there
Among the mingling leaves
That cover the pathways
For love's secrets.

So when spring is over,
And summer is passing,
I will see you once more
In a season of beauty.
Then autumn can rob us
Of all summer's meaning,
But we can be happy
Together again.

Dominic Allard

CLIMBING TO LOVE'S PINNACLE

Whilst I am searching the horizon for you
Looking everywhere except like you do
I sense that warmth, that atmospheric key
Wondering if you are to appear so contented
And happy with me
Whilst we are apart, I daydream of us together,
Rose covered fields and sunny weather
I suppose it's like climbing trees, something that
We will always do
That special feeling since I fell for you
But this is that thing that is best done as a pair
Climbing up high, a view to share
Perched up high, happy at my feat
You climb up to join me, my life feels complete
As we sit there up high watching the setting sun
I wait for that star, to wish for us, to stay as one.

Marcus Fyfeldi

WHEN SPRING IS IN THE AIR

When spring is in the air
There's loving everywhere,
The soaking of the season's thought
There's loads to learn and still to be taught.
The graceful sunrise playing a part,
Helping the feeling down deep in your heart.
Encouraging a special something down deep inside,
A feeling that's not hard it's easy if you try.
Of all emotions I think that love is the king,
Because we all feel more frisky when the seasons change -
To *spring!*

Kieghley Joyce

SPRING

(In dedication to Sylvia my wife, my life)

Spring has returned once again
Weather slightly warmer and a drop of rain
Trees and flowers, preparing to burst out
All of them in their way do shout
Snowdrops and crocuses all gone
For time just keeps rolling on
Nature begins to show her glory
And what a beautiful story
Time is endless, this we know
But spring is part of the show
The nice smell of new ploughed earth
Then you realise what it's all worth
The aroma of fresh cut grass
Lambs frolicking as we pass
The great change is coming as before
And we all know it's the same forever more
The sun's rays, making all life grow
As onward and forward time doth go
Man cannot hope to copy all this
Its beauty and energy pure bliss
Lovers wandering by
But they don't even see the sky
Some spectacular colours now unfold
For all mankind to behold
Part of a master plan they say
And spring brings more beauty every day
New life now growing all around
And bird songs get very loud
I really love this season called spring
For into my old heart comes something.

Prince Rhan

REMEMBER SPRING

When days were short and nights were long,
we yearned for days with birds in song,
with trees that came to life again,
an end to cold, the snow and rain.
Everything seems brighter now
with colours bold in every hue,
it's all out there for me and you.
The sun now shines and days are bright
and nature again has won its fight!
But what of us?
Our hearts can lighten and now can sing
it's the season for love, *yes . . . spring.*
But make the most of every day
while the world seems brighter in every way.
For time doesn't stop for anything,
love and passions come and go
and then they fade like melting snow,
just like the days we had in spring.
Spring and summer pass behind,
the colours are gone, they're hard to find,
and on those dark and endless nights
just think of love and passions too
and all that *spring* now means to you.

Renate Margaretha Jarvis

THE EMERALD VALLEY

The emerald valley, where we lay.
Our bodies warmed by the arresting sun -
Tranquility heightened by birdsong,
The angel chants of the flowing brook -

Here we are careless.
There are no chains to bind our minds
In such an Eden -
Unknowing, our minds set sail for unconsciousness,
To be awakened by the occasional breeze,
That carries the perfume of distant meadows -

I look upon all the fruits arrayed before us.
Within this frame, upon this canvas,
Lies the evidence of creation -
The kindness that gave us the gift of colour
(The valley wears a rainbow crown)
The love that gave us the gift of sound
(Our hearts move to the pastoral symphony) -

And does the stream carry tears of reality?
Do the clouds hold faces that watch over me?
Is my very existence proof to thee?
Is this my solitude,
my emerald valley?

L A Collins

SIGNS OF A SEASON

In furrowed fields,
lone scarecrows stand,
with nothing left to scare.
Bonfires with wood chip smoke,
that lingers in the air.
Falling leaves and acorns,
plump chestnuts for the fire,
blackberries in hedgerows,
a rose hip covered briar.

The smell of ripened apples,
on heavy laden trees,
petals of the last summer rose,
now dance upon a breeze,
with scurrying clouds, migrating birds,
fly hurriedly overhead,
while the hedgehog now in sleepy pose,
curls up in winter bed.
For autumn is upon us,
and she'll lay the land quite bare,
for just around the corner,
is winter's icy stare.

Eileen M Bailey

REFLECTIONS OF A RELATIONSHIP

I'm me
You're you
She's her
They're them.

To go forward
To progress
To evolve
To endure.

Light over dark
Positive over negative
Smiles over tears
Discord over harmony.

Break up.

Barbara Hellewell

SPRING AIR

Spring's a time with all God's blessing
Warm red lips and hands caressing
Country walks with hands a-holding
Moonlit nights love unfolding
Couples run their hearts a-singing
Through a land with bells a-ringing
Air is sweet, bright stars a-shining
This time of year is made for loving
Thank Our Lord for springtime coming.

Matthew Pearson

AWAKENING . . .

Spring blossoms and rebirth memories return reborn,
of summer promise to be and love's dreams drawn.
In reclamation of wonder, senses tune joy in creation.
Jubilant in aliveness,
as in seeing earth each dawn cry tears of dew,
nature's glistening moisture
refreshing the morning world through.
Caught in a cobweb living new light,
jewels its fine thread.
Cupped in awakening flowers dropping,
it drips from opening, smiling heads.
Eventually evaporates in mists fading
into day,
sun's warmth absorbing its coolness away.
I rise from sleep's embrace
night vacates,
and conscious to what surrounds,
I breathe in a new day's breeze.
Receptive to grandeur
in nature's loving touch,
my spirit does ease . . .

Paul Holland

SPRING IS IN THE AIR

Springtime's with us once again
The cold days of winter gone
As night time changes into day
The sun comes up to greet the morn

The blackbird sings to greet the dawn
How sweetly she does sing
The cuckoo sings her lusty song
To herald in the spring

New-born lambs play in the fields
Farmers plant their land
A gentle breeze blows through the trees
Lovers walk hand in hand

It is a wondrous time of year
When all new life begins
Days are warm and sunny
Oh how I love the spring!

Gillian Morrisey

THE LOVELIEST GIRL IN THE WORLD

I can't explain the whens, where's or why's
Your beauty comes as a sweet surprise.
It gives my spirit rise
You are the girl with the loveliest eyes.

I see you everywhere
And in everything
You shine and make my soul sing.
Your beauty is rare
You are the girl with the loveliest hair.

Just to see you
Makes my life worthwhile
To see you I would walk
Mile on mile on mile
You are the girl with the loveliest smile.

We are very good friends
We talk and flirt.
Talk is the means to an end
Somehow you will be my girl
You are the loveliest girl in the world.

Antony Haselton

THE FADED BLOOM

From a host of pretty daffodils,
You selected only one to be your golden prize.
The others quite bowed down,
As she was transfixed in your eyes.

As you gently bent to touch her,
Such magic filled the air
And you made a strange decision,
That for this one, you would care.

She was at her height of beauty,
Set about in full array.
But you feared others to view her,
You were anxious, *would she stay?*

So you plucked her in the prime of life
And kept her to yourself.
You gave her everything she'd need
And set her on a shelf.

Yes, she looked resplendent many a day
As you gazed with loving glance,
But you felt the need to crush her,
It was then, you caused mischance.

For her colour started fading,
Though you gave her more to drink,
Her petals creased to wither
And her spirit seemed to sink.

She was dying right before your eyes,
How were you going to cope?
You had taken everything she had,
You had even taken hope.

Now, she will never see another spring,
She might hardly last the hour.
You ask me 'How do you know so well?'
I, am that poor doomed flower.

Tina Watkin

GALA DAY FAIR

I went to the fair on Gala Day,
Thirty years ago in May.
With Kathleen, June and Mary Sue;
And we all knew what we were going to do.
We went on the swing boats two by two;
Higher and higher in the sky so blue.

Then on to the dodgems to pretend we could drive.
It's a wonder we all came out alive!
We bumped other cars as we sped along;
Dodging and weaving, we could do no wrong.
Next we rode on a switchback, wriggling like a snake.
'Til we had to get off for our stomachs' sake.

A group of lads soon caught our eyes,
And we were in for a big surprise.
We soon paired off, and I made my choice;
An appealing young man with a lovely voice.
We stayed for the fireworks at the end of the day.
Then two by two we went away.

I was lucky, for I fell in love,
With my young man who had fine, fair hair.
We billed and coo-ed like a turtle dove;
And everyone said we made a good pair.
We married, of course, and have a son and heir.
And all because of the Gala Day Fair!

Jean M Senior

SUMMER

I was out walking on a late spring day,
The birds were all singing their own sweet cheerful way
The beautiful daffodil and tulip are fading away,
The young lambs, young no more are making
Their way to countries afar.

The cuckoo is singing over the fields far away,
Come on it's summer, come out and play,
That's what it sounds like to me anyway.
Oh how it lifts the spirit my companion did say,
To see all this beauty on this fine day.
Goodbye to the long dark winter days that
Are so black dark and grey.

Nature takes over with its flower display,
The gardener is in the garden
making sure it stays that way.
For them their labour is in what they see
And the onlooker would agree.
Come on all you people big and small
Come on out and see spring in the fall.
Listen and see what nature says, you will
Know summer is here one and all.

Butterflies, cuckoos and starlings too,
All flying here and there, all doing
Their own thing without a care.
The wind gently blowing and the gardener
Out hoeing, even the ladybird has her job too,
In green leaves and soil she awaits her prey,
For in summer she keeps the greenfly at bay.

The butterfly fluttering indoors and out
What beautiful colours they display
Without a doubt.

Rose Morley

SPRING LOVE

I hope I've sown the seeds of love
In the garden of your heart
You know I've always loved you
Right from the very start.
It started like a rosebud
Its petals were unsealed
And like the rose now open
My love has been revealed
And that some day in the future
You'll give my heart a thrill
By saying that you love me
And answer, not with maybe
But with the words *I will.*

Henry Buxton

RETURN OF SPRING

violet cast the banks and woodland
as the spring returns to haunt
trees and bushes green shoots flourish
and the cuckoo's song is heard
rich the furrowed earth is scattered
with the seeds for life renewed
gambols with the lambs and filters
in the heart of every bird
clearly gurgling runs the river
through the valley down the hill
by the little thatched roof cottage
yielding to the water mill
where the heart now finds seclusion
when the spring returns to dwell

Susan Erskine

SPRING IS IN THE AIR!

I dream out things that all seem clear
When I was young with loads of cheer
I think of the happy times
In the springtime of our lives
That is the sweetest memory on my mind
When people were really loving and kind

Being out and about with Mum and Dad
That is always what made me really glad
To share my springtime when I was young
With the people that I really love
That is what made my life a load of fun
When I was very, very young.

Michelle Barnes

A SILENT MORNING

All looking forward to this time of year
Sun in the sky, singing in your ear
Early in the day the morning dew
Covering the ground, life coming through
All the starlings fighting for food
Sparrows and robins join the brood
The leaves on the trees begin to open
As the cock crows and people are woken
The noise of the traffic drowns the birds
People start moving shouting words
Hustle and bustle all day long
Till nightfall to wait for that song
Feel the power that's all around
Use your perceptions and you'll be found.

David Treciokas

SPRING SONG

Today is the day for dippy duck diving
Splashing and squabbling in the canal.
Water rippling, sun-streaked and dappled,
Triple-rock waved by the waterfowl.

Today is the day for serene swan swimming
Slipping silently over the surface.
Water reflecting sun sleek feathers,
Sculpted wings poised, effortless grace.

Today is the day for quick squirrel climbing
Leaping and flying through the morning sky.
Racing and chasing in new-budded branches,
Hide-and-seek squirrels, tails held high.

Today is the day for happy dog walking
Snuffling and scuffling in crackle brown leaves,
Duck and swan baiting, pouncing and waiting
To be called in to heel and told to behave.

Today is the day to celebrate springtime,
Crisp crackly cold, crystal clear sun.
Reflections so perfect you want to walk into them,
Try out a world gone upside down!

Upside down, dippy duck diving,
Splashing and flashing their feathers around,
Whirling and twirling, flapping and quacking,
Who can help but sing with their joyful sound?

Felicity Howard

SPRINGTIME'S BLESSINGS

O lovely springtime.
All promise now fulfilled.
Your very name makes cares just melt away.
Your sweet air fills our senses,
while our sight
is ever captured by the pure delight
of each more glorious day.

The dark days fade,
and conquered pass away,
while springtime wears her garland of success.
Though winter's chill
preceded first warm light
Spring's fairer power began to win the fight
shown by her brighter dress.

Her leafy woodlands
hear the first glad steps
of those in love, while songbirds serenade.
Primrose and bluebell
spread with carefree ease
their tablecloths of colour round the trees
in every forest glade.

Could beauty last,
would life possess such pain?
Could violence ever triumph over peace?
God knows and understands.
We must obey.
Love triumphs yet and nature still holds sway.
Her joys will never cease.

John Christopher Cole

VALENTINE

O unsuspecting lady of my heart,
You cannot know the havoc that you wreak.
My words self-stifle when they would impart
The feelings which, bewitched, I cannot speak.

Your loveliness, which haunts my wakeful hours
And fills my dreams when day drifts into night,
Casts spells like those of magic secret bowers
Where foolish hopes are turned to dazed delight.

I bring those hopes and lay them at your feet.
'Tis in your power, who artlessly disarms
My heart's defences every time we meet,
To let me sweet-surrender to your charms.

Your victory, achieved without a fight,
Will be both bloodless and - of course - complete.
And I, swift-vanquished, will, sweet queen, be quite
Unquestionably grateful for defeat.

John Slim

THE JOY OF LOVE

Come dance with me and sip the wine
This night is ours, just thine and mine,
Let's taste the heady ecstasy
Tomorrow is still yet to be.
We'll swim the lake in naked bliss
And feel the moonlight's soft caress,
Count stars above to wish upon,
Then capture each and every one.
And as the dawn now comes to light
We'll remember this, our special night,
When summer fades and leaves do fall
This night of love we will recall.

Margaret Malenoir

SPRING IN HEREFORDSHIRE

The earth awakes and suddenly the fields
Take on a newer, fresher green,
Till reluctant winter inevitably yields
Its hold on every passing scene.

The gentle bloom of cherry, plum and pear
Succeeds the earlier white of snow and frost,
While plaintive bleating fills the air
Of new-born lambs, who fear they are lost.

In woods, the primrose's softer gleam
Gives way to bluebells' sapphire blue,
The growing warmth of the sunlight's beam
Stirs the teeming woodland life anew.

The days go by and nature gathers pace
As candle spires light up the chestnut trees,
The verges shimmer, thick with Queen Anne's Lace,
Buttercups, a cloth of gold across the leas.

Lavender and purple, pink and white,
Lilac's heady perfume scents the air,
Laburnum showers glow golden bright,
The sound of birdsongs everywhere.

Where else does beauty seem as real,
So close to touch on every hand?
Our England's gentle quiet appeal
Can vie with any foreign land.

Joan Weston

WHEN THE MAY FLOWERS ARE OUT

'Please sit down' says the guy behind the desk.
I'm at the local garage - the car is in
For an MOT. 'I'll sit, thank you.
And I'll wait.
Till the whole lot's done.'
He asks . . . 'Coffee?' He smiles . . .
I think, coffee, how nice! Is it
. . . usual? Does he offer coffee to everyone?
I smile, and say 'Thank you - yes'

I read a magazine. I hear a horn.
It's her, it's my car . . . will she get through?
The guy behind the desk is eyeing me up -
I swear, he is eyeing me up. I lift my head.
He quickly looks away. Fiddles.
Fiddles - then rests his eyes on me again!
. . . On my legs! More precisely on my legs!
Does it bother me? No . . .
I like it, I admit!
Like it, like it, love it!
I love it, when the may flowers are out,
and guys suffer from spring fever!

I finish my coffee. What's the time?
A mechanic comes in. Says all is in order
To the guy behind the desk.
She got through! I'm not sure I am pleased . . .
It means her and I won't be back!
Shame on me, shame -
After all, I am a married woman!

I drive off. Switch the radio on. My,
It's good to be alive!

Claire-Lyse Sylvester

ENCHANTED SPRING

He was to wear the willow,
on this bleak winter day,
it seemed she had left forever,
and nothing did she say.

He wondered what had happened,
where had his maiden gone,
alas a witch had cast a spell,
and his heart did mourn.

Then one day in spring,
on the lake he saw,
a snow white looking swan,
and to him she called.

His heart beating faster
when he called her name,
and to the waterside the
beauteous swan came.

Like an enchanted spell,
when he kissed her breast,
she turned to human form
the loveliest princess

Rejoicing in such happiness,
to see his love again
they embraced each other,
and flowed the love of spring.

The spell was now broken,
for his love was pure and strong,
they celebrated spring,
with merriment and song.

E Sturdy

THE MAGIC OF SPRING

Awakened by the song of birds,
And snowflakes fluttering by
They'll tell me what I wish to know,
That spring is nigh.

'Twill not be long they seem to say,
As the earth unfolds its treasure,
And the waters ripple once again
Giving us all much pleasure.

The trees had shaken off their gowns,
Of every different hue,
Waiting for the magic touch,
To clothe them all anew.

I saw a chaffinch and a long-tailed tit,
A thrush and starlings three,
A moorhen and a tufted duck
On the river that flows to the sea.

The seagulls shrieked above my head,
White, as snow that was falling,
Swooping up and down, and round about,
And all the birds were calling.

Come and join us they seemed to say,
As I raised my eyes to the sky,
'Twas then I saw the sun rise,
And I wished that I could fly.

To fly away to heaven's gate,
And sing my praises there,
To join the chorus of the birds,
And all the glory share.

Betty Thomson

RENEWAL

Now the dark mornings have passed,
Spring is upon us at last.
Birds they do sing in the trees,
A perfume that hangs in the breeze.
Mother nature it seems is refreshing her dreams,
Sending messages out with the bees.
From the ground burst out flowers,
With the fresh April showers
Bathing each bright new bloom that does please.
Whilst the mother birds flitter,
and the fox has her litter,
The world seems to awake from a sleep,
All of nature obeying, spring games it is playing,
Let's renew life, new promises keep.
For we too are a part of the plan,
We should help out wherever we can,
Remember that flame in your heart,
The bit about death us do part,
Wake up to the world it is spring,
So open your heart up and sing.

K R Griffiths

OVERWHELMING DESIRE

I want your body, I want it bad,
What I want is what I've had.
Closeness and affection 'til the end of time,
Please arouse me and be totally mine.

I love for you to tell me you love me,
I'd die for your touch, can't you see?
The beat of my heart is so fast,
Only when I'm near you does it last.

I cry out to just touch your face,
To look into your eyes, I'm in a different place.
I wish I could climb into your bed,
Completely yours to do whatever you said.

I need you to be as happy as can be,
To appreciate life and especially me.
And I know I would like you to be so near,
But only on the condition, you would love me here.

Lemanie Kelly

FATAL ATTRACTION

Phil has never had much success
With the girls he really sets out to impress
Why, only last week, he was out at a bar
When he noticed this beautiful girl from afar

He thought up a plan, not too perverse
As he sat himself down, in the seat next to hers
First, he dropped his front door keys
And, picking them up, touched both of her knees

When he re-surfaced, she wore a big smile
(Give Phil an inch, and he'll take a mile!)
So the next thing he dropped was a pack of King Size
And on his way up, he felt both her thighs

Her smile grew much bigger, as she asked for a pen
An invite to her place? (thought Phil) but then
She gave him the scribbled-on, beer mat note
Which bore disappointment for Phil, and I quote . . .

'Mind how you go, for my name's Clive
And I'm working undercover, for MI 5!'

Margaret Sanderson

PRIMAVERA

The sun shines high above us,
and little birds that sing
circle round the heavens at
the start of every spring.

The wildlife in the hedgerows
build cosy little homes,
in which to raise their offspring
midst the pixies and the gnomes.

Squirrels hoard their nuts,
and then prepare a drey
wherein their tiny babies
can sleep and eat and play.

Little lambs dance in the fields
sand-coloured, black or white.
Happy frisking creatures
leaping through the light.

Graceful swans glide o'er the lake,
and little cygnets lead
some mallards to the bulrushes
where coots and moorhens breed.

A myriad tiny ants
are bustling to and fro,
building high an anthill
to which their queen must go.

At dawn among the bushes
glow sparkling, shiny gems.
Dewdrops on the spiders' webs
'twined round the flower stems.

There's no more ice and no more snow,
just scented blossoms round us blow.

Daf Richards

ADORATION, A ROSE

A finger of light
Softly touches your face
You talk without words
Define beauty and grace

A temptress of song
And goddess of praise
The crown of emotion
And love's strong embrace

Around you bad thoughts
Always sink without trace
You guide me to love
And bring hope to my days.

Tony Reid

ALL THIS FROM EYES

Those crazy Irish eyes are looking at me,
Burning through me like the midday sun,
Seeping into my mind through my shallow skin,
Into the depths of my body.
All this at just one look,
The power he emits towards me,
I can feel the love, the anger, all the emotions.
He has an aura that makes me want to scream
out loud all the things that peep into my mind,
That make me think, imagine, move, breathe.
Mistakes that I make
Flood back to me,
I do not regret, there is no time
For such trivialities today.
I must move, find my destiny,
It is time to find the owner of those eyes.

Fiona Stimpson

THE SEASONS

Spring is a time for a new beginning
The flowers are blooming, the birds are singing.

Summer is a time for holidays and sunshine
Barbecues in the garden, and having a good time.

Autumn is a time for leaves a-turning
Harvest gathering, grass fires burning.

Winter is a time for rain and snow
Long dark nights, and fires aglow

The festive Yuletide is a special season
Although shorter, it has a reason

A time for families and friends to be together
Caring and sharing, whatever the weather.

Another year ends and the seasons start over
Also, of course, we are another year older

As the world goes round and times do change
The seasons, thankfully, remain the same.

Joy Sanders

LUST OF SPRING

Teasing, setting blossom free
Wind, romping through lazy branches
Cherry white, the joy enhances
In the early morning sunlight

Float as feathers on their journey
Short lived, year in the making
Now the wind, intent on raping
And the cherry left undressed.

Marian Acres

A TOUCH OF SPRING

Clearer skies every morning
The birds sing a merry tune,
Also to awaken the dawn
You feel more lively within yourself,

Trees that have been asleep
Suddenly show more life
With fresh buds appearing,
Little snowdrops,
Rise to the surface of the earth,

And cats once again
seem more active outside,
Climbing trees,
And catching the odd bird,
The odd insect, intrude
Into the house.

And daffodils with their
Fresh springy yellow
Glitter in the spring sunshine,
And everywhere becomes
Green where there are
trees, and gardens,

And occasional rain,
Makes the spring a
Lovely time.

Novello N Maynard-Thompson

WELCOME TO SPRING

Just as March begins to show
Her early flowers unto the world
The bush beside my kitchen window
Its tiny buds it will unfurl

In dark winter its branches bare
Are raised aloft against grey skies
They seem to be offering up a prayer
Of hope, that soon the sap will rise

Yet in summertime, when leaves appear
Its branches spread across the lawn
Providing shade for those dwelling here
To evening's end, from morning's dawn

But spring is when it has its day
The golden flowers glow like the sun
Even when clouds are dark and grey
It sheds its light on everyone

At last, at last, it seems to say
Tossing its blossoms in the sun,
I'll proudly stand here, come what may
Now that spring has really come.

Ann Thomas

INTERLUDE

I hear her tread upon the stair.
See the gleam in her golden hair.
She's coming up to our little love nest.
She always comes at my behest.

Together we enter her bedroom sweet.
Soon her clothes are at her feet.
Our arms entwine, our breaths commingle.
Soon my body begins to tingle.

Together we enter the realms of love.
My hands caress her below and above.
All too soon it is time to rest.
I gently bend down and kiss her breast.

I fold her in my arms - we sleep.
Never was sleep so sweet and deep.
When we wake, we love again.
Then I have to get up to catch my train.

Denys Kendall

LAST WALTZ

I prayed that Cupid's arrow
Would pierce your tender heart,
I prayed that from tomorrow
We'd never be apart;
And now my prayers are answered,
You've come to me in love,
You've fallen for the dancer
Who's as graceful as a dove.

I've tantalised and teased you
Each night upon the floor;
It's good to know I've pleased you
And you're coming back for more,
For when I joined this motley crew,
To learn to ballroom dance
And find a man, at ninety two
I knew 'twas my last chance!

Kay Spurr

SPRINGTIME

Out walking with Bess, my faithful dog!
Seeking observations, plus thoughts, to log!
Time of year; birth of spring!
Place, woodland. Sound; birds, that sing!
Listening contented, in the surround;
To every natural, endearing sound!
Suddenly, a noise above;
That of two birds, making love!
Being latter part, in ageing stage;
Silly thoughts, begin mind engage!
Suppose humans filling passionate desire;
Sought a tree, to quell, their fire!
Imagination; wife and I;
Seeking tree, to comply!
Our age, struggling up the trunk;
End up, falling, with a heavy plunk!

Robert Denham

SPRING IS IN THE AIR

Springtime is that time of year when,
We clasp and greet the lighter weather to cheer
And because our planted bulbs shoot up of every sort,
Crocuses, iris, tulips, and daffodils to warm the heart.

The new-born lambs go gambolling into the fields
They take in the air then get on their heels,
Spring is in the air so they just
Take up the skipping as if they must.

Spring makes us all so frisky, we cannot keep still
Our lungs have been starved so we rush out for refill,
Out goes the foul air and in comes the fresh
We get that youthful feeling we can never forget.

Mary Joseph

LIGHT SUMMER DRESSES

Off to school, today, on the first day of May,
Girls in light summer dresses.
All dressed as one, no-one is outdone
By those light summer dresses.

Conversely the trees are not so at ease
Over light summer dresses.
They dither and stall, and can't agree at all
About light summer dresses.

The beeches are bold for they ignore the cold
In their light summer dresses.
In their wisps of pale green, they're the first to be seen
In their light summer dresses.

The oaks are not so, for they *will not* go
For those light summer dresses.
'Until it *stays* bright, it just isn't right
To wear light summer dresses.'

Opinions are weighed, and some trees are swayed
To wear light summer dresses.
But many will stay until well into May
Without light summer dresses.

Then they'll all go, and stand row upon row
In their light summer dresses.
But it's those first beech leaves on that make us all long
For those light summer dresses.

Ian Hodgkinson

THE BLACKBIRD'S LAMENT

If I were a blackbird I wouldn't whistle or sing!
I'd just sit on my perch, sigh, or not do a thing!
I wouldn't fly to foreign shores,
On the whole they're all such bores!
I'll dine thrice a day on unsuspecting prey,
A worm or two passing my way,
It's the weather you see,
So cold and drear,
Not conducive to a sun lover like me,
And so I sit and ponder my dear,
I! Me! That famous bird of the woods and the glen,
When the sun shines I may well sing then!
What's that I hear? I listen, there's no doubt,
It's a mating call to me! A lady's about!
I preen and I spy the sun high in the sky,
I puff out my chest, well one has to at least try!
She sits beside me, a sweet little thing,
Thank goodness for the seasons, especially, *Spring!*

Joyce M Hefti-Whitney

JUST US TWO

Tender is the night when love is there
Only stars and the fading moon watch
As two lovers' lips their tender moments share
The day's worries forgotten in a loving embrace.
Passion rises as hearts and pulse begin to race
Endearments whispered as lips caress neck and ear
Lost in each other's arms heaven's gates they near
These emotions only lovers share.
When the kaleidoscope of feelings finally spent
Just these two know that love was lying there.

Winifred Wardle

CHERRINGTON LAKE

I saw this tinker in a wood
And passed quite close to where he stood
He raised his cap and scratched his head
And then, quite suddenly, he said
'I fetched this fish out yonder lake
I suppose I am allowed to take.'

I said to him 'I can't see why
You shouldn't have a fish to fry'
But the farmer's mooching round about
With gun in hand, so do look out
And the thing that he cannot stand
Are strangers poaching on his land.

I passed the tinker coming back
He winked and lifting up a sack
And with a rough and hearty laugh
Divided all his fish in half
'Well, thank 'ee ma'am' he said to me
'I hope you too, like fish for tea.'

Helen Bull

SPRING TIME

Spring is the time for lovers
When Cupid plays all his tricks
Spring is the time for the mothers
Of babies and soft fluffy chicks
Spring is the time of renewing
Seed - so the new crops will grow
Spring is the time of the old ones
Giving body and heart a new glow.

Jessie Fradley

A NIGHT OF PASSION

Sitting beside the coal fire, I'm there with you alone,
The flickering light illuminates, the beauty that is your own,
I see your naked shoulders, to where your slender neck sweeps down,
I wouldn't swap your elegance, for the prettiest girl in London town.

I have pulled the blinds together, and from my reclining chair,
I stretch my hands towards you, ensuring you are still there,
I smell your wonderful aroma, it is absolutely sublime,
I feel my pulse is beating, wanting your spirits to mingle with mine.

All my worries disappear, as I put my lips to yours,
I feel your liquid's flowing, like the seas against the shores,
It has given me inspiration, to write another little rhyme,
'Cos you are the tastiest bottle of brandy I've had, in a long long time.

Wenn The Pen

I LOST MY LOVE IN SPRING

Awoke to the sound of spring and clearer skies,
The morning sun's rays dries my tear-stained eyes,
Lush green grass fills the meadows,
Thinking about you, while my head rests on a pillow,
Not even the April showers can wash my blues away,
You walked out of my life, memories of
what we had will always stay.
Night falls, the fading sun will return tomorrow,
I am all alone in the world, with only my sorrows,
The seasons may have changed from winter to spring,
Unlike the birds, my broken heart fails to sing.

Graeme Muir

WHAT SPRING CAN BRING?

I met my true love in the early spring
While migrating birds were still on the wing
We stood hand in hand beneath the willow tree
Where I kissed him and he kissed me
We walked thro' fields with new-born lambs at play
Jumping high to the sky till the end of the day
We walked by a stream picked daisies for chains
Then sheltered under trees from early morning rain
We walked down the lane saw crocuses and snowdrops
New leaves on the trees with blossoms to the top
Newly hatched birds trying hard to fly, with
Fluffy down feathers would they ever reach the sky?
We stood for a moment looked in each other's eyes
Only *our* true love could shame the blue skies
The sky looked bluer the grass more green
The world in spring is the best I've ever seen.
We walk in total silence dreaming of what's to come
Our wedding day not far away, oh look! Here comes the sun.
We pass by a farm at the end of the lane.
It's still very cold 'cos the robin's here again
The cows in the field the pigs in the sty
Little piglets squealing what a wonderful sight
The farmer's field is furrowed ready to be sown
Love seems to blossom in spring from a seed all of its own
New life emerges animals birds and flowers
My love and I in spring spend many happy hours
Quite soon we'll be together for ever and a day
Thank you to the spring for sending you my way
Spring really has sprung, hooray, hooray, hooray!
But next time we walk down the lane, what will
Happen, who can say?

Sandra Witt

SPRING DREAMS

My love and I, on a journey have been
I will tell you now of things we have seen.
But first I must say that it is spring.
We wandered slowly hand in hand
Went in a park listened to a band,
Looked at the blossom and flowers so sweet
Appreciated love and dreams that were ours,
So long ago we did exchange our vows.
We see young lovers, having a kiss and cuddle,
And we hope that their lives they'd never muddle.

In spring our thoughts they turn to love,
To nice warm breezes and turtle doves.
The bracken soft, trees whisper low
We all think through life with love we will go
But I will tell you now our sweet love song.
My love's eighty three - and I'm eighty one.
Our love from us has never gone
So I know for sure it will go on.

Mildred Doreen Jacomb

JOYOUS SPRING

Shake us from the bonds of winter,
Cold dark nights and freezing rain,
Fill our hearts with joyous springtime,
When nature starts to live again.

Buds surge forth in splendid glory,
Shrubs and trees burst into leaf,
Daffodils, primrose, tell the story,
Catkins' tails, it must be spring.

Birds cavort in courtship dances,
Blackbird's song it fills the air,
Trees with blossom, heavy laden,
Lambs that frolic without a care.

Now the days are getting longer,
Feel the warming of the sun,
Cuckoos call from distant woodland,
Oh how I love when spring has sprung.

John Bendle

SPRING IS IN THE AIR

Spring is here and oh what fun
The lambs are having in the sun
Up the hills and down the dales
Stop to drink and shake their tails
In the woods the primroses peep
Waking from their winter's sleep
Little rabbits scampering by
And in their dens young foxes lie
In the garden snowdrops white
Come to life with the aconite
Crocuses both blue and gold
Daffodils like soldiers bold
Now's the time to sow the seeds
Of vegetables for winter needs
Flowers bright to give you pleasure
And memories that you can treasure
So this is spring for all to see
And all of this to us is free.

Jessie Bishop

AWAKENING

Through the isolated winter
Where do your thoughts go?
Into the river of hibernation they flow
At rest they stay
Lost in the darkness
Of every cold day

Spring, slowly begins to bud
And creative thoughts begin
To bloom and creep
Through your blood

Shake off the cobwebs
In your dusty mind
And let your soul begin to shine
With the inspirations
Of all around you see
Through spring's reality

Children's laughter fills the air
Grass cutter humming
Ice-cream vans jingling at the fair
Dogs barking, wildlife squawking
Barbecues smouldering, aromas so fine
All these things erupt in your mind
Accompanying the emotions of spring time.

Sandra Ford

YOU'RE THE REASON I FELL IN LOVE

You're the key to open the door.
You're the dream from the night before.
You're the flame burning on the candle.
You're the hand that turns the handle.
You're the water to fill the cup.
You're the legs that hold me up.
You're the salt from the sea.
You're the honey from the bee.
You're the picture hanging on the wall.
You're the graze left from the fall.
You're the apple in my tart.
You're the pounding beat in my heart.
You're the tears formed when I cry.
But you're the reason I always ask why?
Why are we now apart from each other?
Why do we seem to drift further and further?
Why is there always someone better?
She made you break my heart, why did I let her?
Why don't you listen when I always insist?
Why can't I just forget you even exist?
I'll tell you why I can't forget.
Because something happened the first time we met.
It's not hard to figure out the answer to the above
It's easy to explain . . . *I fell in love!*

Laura McMeikan

SUDDEN RAPTURE . . .

Yesterday, all was cold and bleak.
Then, with a whisper, a creak
All came to life. Everything
From Nature's well. It is spring.
There, there on grasses green
With lush blades to be seen
Is dandelion's yellow scattered fair.
Hawthorn's blossom fills the air;
Fleeing before a sudden squall.
Spring's sprung upon us all.

Amazed people summer clothes tout;
Rapturous laughter's all about
As leaves then creep upon the twig
And nature's well saps a sprig.
Bare, bare in winter's cold
Spring explodes colours bold
With squalls of laughter that peel the air
Of cold restraint dying there;
Fading within this abrupt pall.
Spring's sprung upon us all.

Relief, sudden rapture are bared
And sprung spring is with people flared
As they clock the cuckoo's time-call;
With cries of glee, they enthral.
Here, here the spring's skies blue
With flush clouds rains construe
And prisms for rainbows to arc then light;
A pot of gold comes to sight.
Reaping the gold abundant there,
Nature's love-bird trills to pair.

Flattered landscape engenders sighs.
Winter's bare-boned skeleton dies.
There, there winter's wrung.
Here, here spring is sprung.
Bare, bare yesterday.
But, but not today . . .

Lloyd Carley-West

SPRING

The winter thaw has trickled by
Dawn unfolds, the wake is nigh
Spring unfurls its great, green belt
The cleansing sun is warmly felt.

Spires of blossom proudly throng
Woodlands and dales burst with song
Sweet, fragrant flowers parading in prime
Glimpse the first cuckoo arriving on time.

Rainbow glories arc the sky
Hedgerows glisten, borders sigh
The long sleep over animals rejoice
Bustling and mating in true country voice.

The regal robin on his throne
Surveys his kingdom for a home
Farmers haul their faithful plough
Rookeries bend every bough.

Laughter embellishes children at play
Lambs on the hillside have plenty to say
The landscape is haunted by grandeur and fun
Sublimely created, blissfully done.

D P Elliott

SPRING

Give way thou cold and wintry blast
I know the spring has come at last
No more we're chilled from top to toe
When these blizzards cease to blow.

Now we see a feast of flowers
Glowing in every garden bowers
Never a rainbow shone so bright
Or the moon her brilliant light

Nothing really can compare
To the colours we see there
Or the wonders to be found
In a piece of garden ground.

Barbara Dearness

WILD HORSES

Depart from the shadows, engage in the light,
Come run away with me, into the night,
For as wild horses we will then be,
So contented and satisfied, so utterly free.

Keeping our wants and desires, within our sight,
While remembering always, to hold on tight,
For as wild horses, we will then be,
So vivacious, excitable, and totally free.

Wandering from the darkness, we'll take the path that is bright,
The path of togetherness, so beautiful and right,
For as wild horses, we will then be,
So contented and satisfied, so utterly free.

Rachel Demet

THUNDER

I was burning with desire
Like some overwhelming fire
And my heart was beating like thunder

My body trembled at your touch
Your tender kisses meant so much,
And my heart was beating like thunder.

I listened closely to your voice
When you were here, I had no choice
And my heart was beating like thunder.

Since that first day I heard your name
My life has never been the same
And my heart was beating like thunder.

I loved you true, I love you still,
I guess you know I always will
And my heart was beating like thunder.

Jennifer Emery

WONDERFUL DAY

It was a wonderful day,
the sky was blue, the sun shone,
I felt its warmth on my face.
Flowers all around,
birdsong, I felt thankful for the approach of spring,
for peace and tranquility, the sweet, fresh air,
and for the love, and companionship I have,
thankful for the joy that spring brings forth,
thankful for life itself.

John Anderson

WEAKENING WINTER AND STRENGTHENING SPRING

It is as shameful, as much of a sin as to trample
On January's aconites; to spoil joy
When the winter grows weak, and spring signs gather force.
To feel firm woodland soil is delight worth the sample.
Then, celandines wake in a spirit of 'Attaboy!'
A challenge accepted by ivy and gorse.

Patterns of branches without leaves flit by me, like
Upside-down lightning, in umber, not silver-white.
Snowdrops in gardens rise, then thumb bud-noses at
Winter, and treat it with scathing scorn and dislike.
Sunshine banishes moping moods; works to incite
Us to idleness, lingering and friendly chat.

Gillian G Fisher

WELCOME SPRING

March winds blow and we may get some snow
Followed by April rains - and we know
That spring is not far away, we can feel it in the air
The time of year for love and romance is everywhere.

Lambs in the fields are gambolling too
Making us feel frisky - but that's nothing new
Lovers strolling hand in hand in the park
Waiting for the day to end and love in the dark.

Buds on the trees burst forth and bloom
Goodbye to winter and doom and gloom
Welcome spring so glad you are near
The season of love is once again here.

Marjorie Ridley

THE SPRINGTIME KISS

Through all the seasons of the year
I admired you constantly.
Yet the words remained unspoken,
For this love could never be.

Your life and mine so different
That our paths would never meet,
You were gentle, charismatic,
Professionally elite.

Then one May morn we met by chance
In a quiet wooded chine.
We walked, and talked of many things,
I adored your voice divine.

Here, at last we stood together,
Your eyes burned deep into mine.
Nothing could separate us now
As I touched your face so fine.

You drew me so close, and held me
As our lips met in a kiss.
I wished it would last forever,
For nothing had been like this.

My heart was pounding so wildly,
More than real it all did seem.
But suddenly then, I woke up!
It was a *lovely* dream.

Patricia Thomas

THE MOOD FOR LOVE

As the pale yellow moon rises above
And turtle doves spread the song of love,
Many lonely rivers drift to the sea
As spring draws near to you and me.

Nature can feel the powerful pulsing of love in my vein
As butterfly tears whisper your name.
Love is a mirror which holds your reflection
While the spring mood is an incurable infection!

We rollick together in a buttercup meadow
And a pile of daisies jointly we sew.
Above us trees of blue, pink and yellow -
Blossom is spring's way of saying 'Hello.'

Spring evokes a fiery passion
Which blinds me to an unknown fashion.
Love is tamed by your unspoken words
That I read in your eyes and my soul heard.
The season of spring restores youthful powers
So romance flourishes with every passing hour
It blooms like a rose without thorns,
Every sunrise to sunset a new sensation is born.

Angeline Joffe

ARRIVAL OF SPRING

In the spring white clouds bring, a softening of frosty airs,
Like speeding boats with rounded sails they gaily cross the blue,
They seem to say - 'It's spring today, we bring a precious cargo
Of milder days and warming showers and early morning dews.'

So once again the sun and rain raise the sap in dormant stems,
New shoots appear like magic in the tenderest shades of green;
Amidst the showers spring's early flowers race to show their faces
And soon the whole gay world of colour is competing to be seen.

In the fields on moors and wealds the spirit of new life is seen,
Little lambs are gambolling with woolly tails a-quiver,
While in the hedges, banks and sedges, young nestlings being hatched
Prove new life is breaking out from mountain side to river.

The human breast too feels the zest of rising, thrusting force,
Fresh appetite for living surges upward through our veins,
The clouds we've seen and shoots of green and colour everywhere
Have raised an echo in ourselves - those springtime clouds and rains!

Ken Whitten

SPRING - THE AWAKENING

The long winter slumber is past.
Gone is the wind's chill blast.
Warm air replaces cold.
New growth replaces old.
The snow goes.
Fresh green grass glows.
Daffodils and crocuses arise
And peer upward to the blue skies.
Birds take to the wing,
Excitedly they chatter and sing,
To welcome the coming of spring.
Hares leap and rabbits run.
Soon all the animals join in the fun,
And the earth throbs in the spring sun.
Trees once gaunt and bare,
Bright new leaves now they share.
Waters once frozen gurgle with delight,
And fish dart in and out of sight.
People move with lighter tread.
Now it's easier to get out of bed.
The warm sun beckons to them all.
Now it's springtime, let's have a ball.

John V Ford

CUCKOO TIME

I heard the cuckoo this morning
Across the fields far away
A strange sound this spring day
Just as the day was dawning

Spring has come at last
Primroses with their creamy yellow
A subtle perfume and colour so mellow
Behind us is the winter's blast

Baby lambs are being born
In fields where grass is now so green
And covered with a dewy sheen
Where some were born at dawn

The gardener in me begins to awaken
Planning all the seeds to sow
Then the lawn I will have to mow
My lethargy will have to be shaken

Off to the garden centre I go
Like a kid in a toy shop
Never know when to stop
Planning the plants to put in a row

Flowers in pink and blue
Rambling, spreading and tall
Some to climb the garden wall
Of every single shade and hue

Cabbages, beans and peas
Soon will be sprouting in the ground
Potatoes covered with a mound
Any left shall have to freeze.

Jennifer Laidlaw

SPRINGTIME

Oh to be young when spring is in the air
Life's full of promise, you haven't a care
The air is scented with blossoms anew
The smell of fresh grass fills the air
Daffodils nod off without a care
Walks in the park, the boat lake alive
With new little ducklings trying to survive
Lovers stroll hand in hand, hearts fit to burst
Hoping love will blossom with love that is true
The world has come alive, looking fresh and new
Spring's comes like a breath of fresh air
Colours vibrant beyond compare
Greens, blue, different hues
Nature calling sure and true
The lush, the green, the perfume,
A wonderful world, everything's in bloom
Bluebells nod in springtime breeze
Nestling snugly near the trees
Everything is all aglow
Nature busy, after winter snow
A beautiful world as spring transforms
Vibrant in colour, the earth re-born
Birds busy twittering, everything alive
As mother nature once more survives
The warmth in the air, you can feel its glow
Nature comes alive and all should know.

Irene Pearce

WE JUST CLICKED

Reached the Roxy about a quarter to nine
In the purple drapes, with a mate of mine.
Strolled past the bouncer with the deadly kick.
Eyes fast searchin' for a pretty chick.
At the soda bar, she struck a pose
With blonde ponytail, and scarlet bows.
She was picked - for legs divine.
She was picked - for her slim line.
She was picked - she'd do me fine. She was picked.

Steered black suede creepers to this choice of mine.
Still partin' the grease on the DA fine.
Said 'Hi pretty baby, let's twinkle the toes,
Let's cut a rug as we twist the hose.'
When she looked at me with big blue eyes.
Two jelly legs wobbled with surprise.
We just clicked - love at first sight
We just clicked - two hearts took flight.
We just clicked - pink stars shone bright. We just clicked.

We rocked with frenzy till it struck midnight,
'Neath crystal balls tryin' to ruin the sight.
As Jerry sung we really had a ball.
This groovy chick really gave her all.
Then as two straws shared one lemonade,
This ten-foot guy knew he had it made.
We just clicked - sweet bluebirds sang.
We just clicked - love's bow went twang.
We just clicked - fireworks went bang. We just clicked.

Said 'Hey pretty babe can I see you home?'
The hot-rod's grounded, but these feet will roam.
We could crash at Ricky's for a bite to eat
The world's our oyster, if the funds can meet.'

I held her purse while she powdered her nose.
Then hit the street as the full moon rose.
We just clicked - I'm hers, she's mine.
We just clicked - now bells will chime.
We just clicked - we'll rock through time. We just clicked.

Violet M Corlett

I DREAMED A DREAM

I dreamed a dream it was of you
To hold you 'neath the sky so blue
To run my fingers through your hair
To kiss your lips and skin so fair

Your eyes so gentle but never cruel
They glint and sparkle like any jewel
Our two hearts beat as if in time
As our bodies start to entwine

Like many fireworks in the night
Your body starts to come alight
All your body starts to glow
It comes across you from head to toe

My love for you is all consuming
Like a flower my love is always blooming
Come lay beside me, love be mine
Let us always cherish this moment in time

I dreamed a dream it was of you
Making love 'neath the sky so blue
If this is heaven I'll gladly stay
With you, I'll while my life away

Fay Stanton

WINTER'S FAREWELL

The trees turned gold for a second,
Blazed to life in the early spring sun,
As bold summer beckoned,
The world, pale and wan
From black winter's chill,
Stirred in anticipation
of June days that fill us
With joy, exultation:
Food, fresh air and wine,
Forget snow, hail and drizzle,
While the weather stays fine,
Hear the barbecue sizzle,
The dancing gnats whine.
One brief moment, that's all,
Then the trees once more black,
Stood like skeletons tall,
Kill-joy winter was back
On this first day of spring,
Snarling death bed 'Goodbyes.'
But short-lived now his sting!
Caw black crows, blue magpies,
Squabbling hags in the Bury March skies.

Alan Swift

DON'T WORRY

This young man asked me a question today
Will I become just like you old and grey.
Will my face have whiskers that will sprout and grow
Then will my forehead have those large busy eyebrows?

I answered him, and said softy don't worry son
You will find out that you won't be the only one.
Then he asked me again will my health last long
I couldn't answer him in case I got it wrong.

Will I have to wear those ugly plastic glasses on my nose
Or will I have those painful corns upon my toes.
Then he said will I go bald and lose my hair
I answered him and said lad you find life isn't fair.

Then he asked me will I make lots of friends
I told him there will be a good one when your life ends
My final answer to him was don't be so worried son
You will find out you won't be the only one.

J F Grainger

MIDNIGHT LOVER

A shaft of moonlight pierces the gloom,
As I lay drowsing in my room.
A voice is whispering, calling me.
I know it's him, I don't need to see.

Softly, seductively he speaks,
To wake me from my fitful sleep.
His touch is like a raging fire,
Filling me with wild desire.

His kisses set my soul aflame,
And between each one he whispers my name.
My body melts as he caresses me,
He makes me his and my mind flows free.

We reach the planets, stars and moon,
Then return to our earthly selves too soon.
I gently stroke his face, then keep
A silent vigil as he sleeps.

He leaves me just before daylight,
With a promise he'll see me again tonight.
A lingering, sensual kiss goodbye,
And I greet the day with a contented sigh.

Catya Shapcott

THE LIGHTER HEARTS OF SPRING

As we emerge from the dark of winter's wood
into the stirring light of spring
the flutter of young hearts begin
and new love spreads its wing.

The lilt of laughter fills the air
and magic is the sound
to the courting couples, arm in arm
showing off the love they've found.

Although their eyes are only for each other
eyes filled with tenderness
as they cuddle one another
with tender love's caress.

They feed upon the food that's love
seasoned with the bloom of early flowers
that makes the heart so tender
and the mind oblivious of showers.

After nature's seeming slumber
in the dark months of winter, drear
hearts seem to be so much lighter
now the time of spring is here.

Danny Pyle

SPRING

Spring is in the air,
The yellow daffodils are dancing here.
The earth no longer is grey and bare,
With tiny flowers beginning to appear.

Spring is in the air,
Colourful tulips are here in array,
Ringing their bells without any care,
Leading us in to wonderful May.

Spring is in the air,
When the trees awaken from their sleep,
Showing their greens so delicate and rare,
Buds, leaves and blossom beginning to peep.

Spring is in the air,
When lads and lasses their rituals begin,
Seeking each other to make up a pair,
Hoping their relationship is one to win.

Alwyn Hall

A SPLASH OF APRIL RAIN

I want him now forever
Never letting go of me
Holding me
Making an everlasting show of me
Shaping and moulding me
His one touch one caress
Then I can feel blessed
From his manly lips
His willing kiss
Yet the rain falls down
It soothes and calms me
Prevents all kinds of harm to me
I could feel so cold and so wet
But I'm not I'm welcoming unable to fret
The soaked skin lets me breathe
The skies open up
Leave me fresh from disease
The rain trickles down my face
Refreshing my existence my own place
The cooling bliss
April rain makes me clean
From blues and solemn pain
I pray upon a splash of April rain.

Jadene Gallagher

GYPSY

The evening scene was tranquil; still,
As sundown stroked the barley mill.
The peaceful stream crept through the trees
And swallow song danced on the breeze.

With looks of tawny vagrant shade,
She gazed across the meadow glade,
And pouting in the sunset fire,
The gypsy eyed her true desire.

The farm lad stacking bales of hay
Was to the gypsy, wanton prey.
His brow was sweating in the heat,
His topless body - rich and sleek.

Her beauty held him mesmerised -
Long auburn locks and chestnut eyes.
Rich crimson lips with bronzen skin
And scarlet nails that beckoned him.

Besotted by her sensual charm,
The farm lad took the gypsy's arm,
And searched the beauty of her form
On velvet fern betwixt the corn.

The evening passed with deep embrace,
Then with a smile upon her face,
She slowly tied her bodice braid
And with a glance, she walked away.

And through the heathered twilight musk,
She disappeared into the dusk.
Another captured by her spell,
The act that gypsy knew so well.

Lynda Ann Green

THE ORCHARD

I wander slowly through the orchard, for this is my last goodbye
We've grown old in the years together, my lovely trees and I
It is only a small apple orchard with but a single cherry tree
A cherry tree so special for the memories rich it holds for me

My brother and I and the boy next door when we were young, we played
Through the halcyon days of summer in its all embracing shade
On my swing I flew through the leafiness as light as a lapwing's feather
And climbed with the boys to the highest boughs for the cherries we
picked together

The blossom in spring matched our innocence, shining like virgin snow
And we felt that we were immortal in those days so long ago
A leaf touches my face as it floats to the ground like a lover's kiss
from the past
And I remember the boy next door and his kisses as he held me fast

I touch every tree in passing, bidding each a silent farewell
But pausing beneath my cherry tree my feelings I cannot quell
Here's where I held my baby, where he reached for the cherries above
His blue eyes sparkling with pleasure, secure in the warmth of my love

Breaking the orchard's stillness comes a swift gust of autumn breeze
From the branches above slowly flutters down the dying brittle leaves
Wafer thin and dimly golden whispering secretly on their way
:Like ghostly childhood voices calling from a long forgotten day

I murmur goodbye to the orchard where my happiest hours were spent
With those I loved, in joy and peace, in our world of sweet content
I say goodbye to my cherry tree and its last leaf falls on my hand
Like a blessing as I leave forever for another, unknown land.

Marianne Cain

COLOUR OF LIFE

I can smell the spring
I'm sure you can
Too.
Little green shoots into daffodils
Will bloom.
Snowdrops and violets
Primroses - abound.
Brown earth pulsating
Fairy rings true.
We welcome the pale sun
As it moves into view.

Nature tells her story
Fresh and new.
Bringing the colour
Of life
Just for you.
I can smell the spring
I know that you
Will too.

Louise Hammett

SPRING FEVER

'In the spring a young man's fancy
Lightly turns to thoughts of love'
We know this saying very well
Two cooing turtle doves

All the wild creatures
Are looking for a mate
Birds are nesting in the trees
They lay their eggs and wait

Spring gives promise of new life
The earth is rich and green
Season follows season
Part of God's great scheme

Give thanks to our Creator
Who takes care of all our needs
Without His love to see us through
We would be poor indeed.

Val Guttridge

FOREVER

The garden was a masterpiece of green and blue and gold,
Excitement welled up in her breast, although her heart was cold,
When April sings, the world awakes and young men seek a mate,
And suddenly she saw him standing at the garden gate.
The vision was so clear to her, and memories returned
So gladly in her mind, that her trembling body burned,
Eager for the passion and excitement of the past
Yielding to his kisses, and swearing love would last . . .

forever.

She turned around and went inside and saw him sitting there,
She went and sat upon his knee and stroked his greying hair,
She saw the question in his eyes and heard him gently say
Thank you for coming back to me, I thought you'd gone away,
A flush came in her cheeks, and a little pang of guilt,
Could a dream betray the trusting love that they had built?
No, spring, and all its passions are all too quickly gone
But the gentle love of autumn, will always linger on . . .

forever.

Roma Court

A LITTLE LAMB

I've just been born a little lamb
To frolic and to leap.
But when I grow up like my mom
I'll be a docile sheep.

It's nice and warm and sunny now
The grass is oh so green.
Is that a full grown cow o'er there
It's the first I've ever seen.

We lambs in meadow run around
We even chase the hens.
King of the Castle is great fun
Also running round the pens.

I've got a nice long tail right now
On it farmers put a band.
And as I grow in weeks to come
It falls off on the land.

Like mom a short tail then I'll have
And woollen coat I'll grow.
And once a year in summertime
They shear it off you know.

Each day a sheep dog rounds us up
The farmer looks us over.
Will we stay here in Eng-e-land
Or do we go to Dover?

I may be sent to market place
And sold with my best mate.
P'raps bought by farmer from afar
Or end up on a plate.

For lambs, life is uncertain
Especially if you're caught.
Will I grow old like my old mom
Or will my life be short?

Geoff Rivers

LIFE (OR AS IT SHOULD BE)

Try to cool down or chill out
Just lay back or select a pew
That's what life is all about
See beyond your own point of view

Have a life, do not really dwell
On things you cannot possibly know
Keep your counsel and do not tell
Secrets that should remain, just so!

Life's too short to really bother
Why do so now you're a little older
Come out of your shell with some sang-froid
And try to become a little bolder

The current fad is *to find oneself*
But introspection leads to loss of confidence
Forget it, enjoy your life, just be yourself
Lay back, be cool, and have some common-sense

Life's a burden, they have been known to say
It can be so if it is lived that way
As Kipling states 'Treat them all the same'
Then you'll find life an exhilarating game.

Ronald John Truscott

TAKE ME . . .

Take me to a place, where I can be,
The person I am, wild and free,
Take me to a place, where passion lies,
And the fruits of heaven, won't pass me by,
Take me to a place, where I can be bare,
A place of purity, that hasn't been shared,
Take me to a place, where I can breath,
All that I taste, and all that I see,
Take me to a place, where my fingers can touch,
The softness of air, fresh and lush,
Take me to a place, that will grasp my heart,
That of a structure, a piece of art,
Take me to a place, where I can feel,
The satisfactions, that pleasure can heal,
Take me to a place, where I can desire,
Every red flame, and the heat of the fire,
Take me to a place, where I've not laid my head,
And words that were thoughts, can be said,
Take me to a place, that is brand new,
A place provided, for me and you.

Sharon Harwood

THE JOY OF SPRING

Spring is the season of joy and happiness,
When the days are filled with peaceful loveliness,
And the air has a hint of the pleasant smell
Of the daffodil and the shy bluebell.

In the spring I can watch a prancing lamb
Darting back and forth between sheep and ram,
And as I merrily skip along,
My heart is humming a joyful spring song.

Ffion Dewi (12)

SPRINGTIME '83

The springtime of eighty three
I vividly recall
the season's flowers in fine array
near the laughing waterfall.

I saw you for the first time.
It was at the Maytime fair
your smiling face your sparkling eyes
your sun-kissed flowing hair.

I made my way towards you
amid the maddening crowd.
Just to be near you
that's all, was on my mind.

My hand reached out and touched you
you proudly turned around
and spoke 'Hello' so softly
my heart began to pound.

I knew there, at that moment
your warmth, your grace, your charm,
that I had found my heaven, on earth
when I held you in my arms.

Stephen Paul McCann

COURTSHIP

There's some lovely young ladies in Newark town,
They are easy to spot if you have been around,
Having travelled abroad, I know what I mean,
Blondes, redheads, and those in-between.

Fair skin, blue eyes, and soft rosy cheeks,
Well dressed, and spoken, and not a bit meek,
So take note you young men if you want a date,
Take along some nice flowers, and don't be late.

It's so hard to be courting for two today,
With so few jobs, and so little pay.
But give it a chance, and do your best,
Who knows, you may come out ahead of the rest.

Think like a partnership, made only for two,
Have a few laughs, don't feel sad or blue,
Work hard together through thick and thin,
Persevere is the word, and you are bound to win.

Rules to remember, are simply this,
Start each new day with a loving kiss.
As your loved one goes out of the door,
Stay happily married forever more.

Michael John Swain

THE TRYSTING-TREE

O who will fondly walk awhile
When buttercups blow free,
My darlings from the village green
Come try the trysting-tree.

O who will coyly spoon with me
This promised spring-tide eve -
Will Joan or Jill or Abigail
Their spells of longing weave?

Hurry now my pretty eyes
And tell me strong and straight,
For I, like every willing lad,
Care nought for girls who wait.

Beneath the trysting-tree, alas
They gave their answer true -
'When I consent to be your bride
Then I will follow you.'

A P Dixon

TRUE LOVE

In different countries we both live
Always return this love I give
For I know I love you true
Please return, what I give to you.

To hear your voice makes my heart sing
How I pray for the phone to ring.
Though I know you can't be near
It is your voice, I long to hear

Day in day out I'll sit and wait
To be with you on a special date
I know this love is very true
How I long to be with you

We both know that through the years
This love of ours has shed some tears
We'll look to the future and not the past
We know our love, forever will last

In this world there's got to be
A special place for you and me
Though we are so far apart
You are always in my heart

Dennis N Davies

THE WALK

Taking a stroll
a walk with a loved one
holding hands
a kiss and an embrace.
All of the scenery,
looks quite picturesque
the weather is warm even though fresh.
Baby lambs some new-born,
jumping and playing
a happy new dawn.
Flowers are blooming
blossoms on trees,
wonderful colours
busy bumble bees.
Birds with their partners
flying the skies
making their love nests
ready for their young.
The sound of the cuckoo
from dawn until dusk,
lovers embracing
with needful must.
The newness of spring
bringing new birth and joy,
love on the earth
seems to spread and multiply.

Jacqueline Williams

PICTURES OF SPRING

Purple spots among the green,
They're here again.
Newly washed by fresh spring rain
Just down the lane.

You have to step off the path
And search for them;
Tiny blooms on slender stems,
Each one a gem.

Beneath shady undergrowth
They lowly lie,
Missed by unobservant eye
Too quick, pass by.

With modesty they arrive,
Their month is May,
When they've served their short-lived day,
They slip away.

They're like little princesses
In purple gowns,
Dainty heads bob up and down,
Deserving crowns.

I used to love the cool air
Brushing me green,
As spring burst upon the scene,
So fresh and clean.

Now I can't get down the lane,
So I just look
At the violets in my book
Of snaps I took.

Mary Care

IN SPRING

Would that I could whisper
Of the feelings you impart.
A presence ever gentle
In my life, my soul, my heart.
Existence is a yearning
Ever longing for you near.
Your image a reflection
In the mirror of a tear.
You are the earth, the sea, the sky
Each sight that I behold.
You are the sun, the wind, the rain
My senses to unfold.
A love still free to blossom
Never shackled by a ring,
Ever rampant deep within me
But especially in spring . . .

Lynda M Bourne

LOVE

The basic love is corrupted
Consumerism kills us all
The ones with love are left out
They refuse to question
What they are about
No love for them
Innocent death
No light for them
A life's regret
Be nothing
Say nothing
Do nothing
Death!

Stephen Adams

SPRING

The beauty of Spring we hold with a reverence
As lambs skip and frolic in the fields.
Refreshed with nature's hope
Yielding to the sun and meadows sweet.
When Spring joins in the frivolity of a young man's laugh
As he wends his way to meet his lass
Her eyes as blue as the sun-kissed sky.
Through the woodland carpeted in blue
Oh! The bluebells, like virtuous maids
You hide your faces from our view.
The innocence of the gentle primrose
As it peeps from within its home of moss
So fine it twines amidst its common lair
So short its time to spare.
Down to the meadow, across the lazy stile
To the babbling brook, its treasures edged with brightest gold
The celandine such beauty to behold.
We reached the aged oak where for centuries had nobly rest
Countless stories it must hold,
Where boughs are mossed and lichen cleave
The high top bare with dry antiquity.
Its hidden grotto that had sheltered
Shepherds and lovers from the sudden April showers
Such long sweet discourse did they hold.
Spring - nature's awakening, refreshes sight and soul
Such pleasure doth it hold.

Anne Christabel Davey-Young

A NEW MAN FOR SPRING

Spring has come summer's drawing near.
I can hear the birds they bring great cheer.
For spring has brought not only the young to their nest.
But the thing that I love best.
New hopes, new dreams, a new beginning to my life.
The end of the pain the trouble and strife.
Spring has brought new love to this lonely heart.
Making the clouds and shadows of the past depart.

My heart is dancing as the lambs in the field,
As to the feelings of youth my spirit does yield.
My heart is learning to fly with mother nature's young
I have done with my winter her songs are now sung.
The old songs of sadness no longer I sing.
For new songs of joy this love now does bring.
Songs of hope, songs of joy, songs of youth.
Song for the new day in search of the truth.

Brightness and sunrises in this valley of green.
Pleasures and peace and new things unseen.
Youth in old age dancing again.
For gone are the tears and the dark years of pain.
This new love is the strength for happy tomorrows.
It pulls the final curtain down on my stage of sorrows.
It is a new day a new time of cheer.
He came with the spring now I know no fear.

Gillian Britton

SPRINGTIME LOVE

There is a very special place where all my dreams come true.
Where the grass and the trees are the deepest green and the sky is a brilliant blue.

As we strolled down the road with its banks of springtime flowers
We stood beneath an old oak tree to shelter from the showers.
When at last the rain stopped and the sun peeped through again
Together we walked hand in hand down the road to memory lane
The chestnut tree's still standing there where I had carved your name.
It was so many years ago but it all looks just the same.
My memories came flooding back to that day so long ago,
When I took your hand and said to you there is something I must know.
I asked if you would marry me if you would be my wife.
And to share the good and bad times that you have in life.
When you said that you would marry me my heart began to sing
For soon we would be married and you would wear my ring.

Albert J Wakeford

SPRING IN THE AIR

The sun is a-shine in the sky now
The birds sing a hymn to the dawn
The crocus has opened her eye now
Her golden head peeps through the lawn.
The swallow now homeward is flying
And rippling again is the burn
For soon where the dead leaves are lying
The bluebells once more will return.
Now spring is here, the winter's through
The night is gone
See the morn breaks anew
Wake my love to the birds' song at dawn
Hope smileth now springtime is born.

Joan Carvell

SPRING

Like a carpet they lay
Beneath the trees
Dancing and swaying
In the breeze
With trumpets of gold
They herald the spring
With trees full of bud
And birds start to sing.
All things in life
Are starting anew
A new beginning
For me and you
These are the gifts
Bestowed with love
Given quite freely
From God above.

Iris Pointon

THE SOURCE

The force that clothes a million fields in green,
That tunes the choirs of birds their songs to trill,
That warms with spring-born flowers the wintry scene,
And frames in blue the distant tree-lined hill.

The power that conjures sights to stir the soul,
Where nature makes her calming presence felt
An omnipresence, sovereign over all,
Before whose visual glory we have knelt.

The source of life that prompts the friendly sun,
The mystic power that wields the magic rod,
The flux that welds all nature into one,
That *force*, that *power,* that *source,* is surely *God!*

Tom Brookman

AS COURTING COUPLES KISS

Come out you love birds
and spread those wings.
Join in with the chorus
as the songthrush sings.

Then step over saplings
so green and new
Playful are the lambs
bleating in pasture's dew.

Dance around fruit trees
on a breeze so light.
Feel the sprinkling of blossom
in pink and white.

Line up with the bluebells
perfectly placed primrose.
Link daisies in a circle
where forget-me-nots show

Slide into meadows
in springtime bliss!
Rabbits are a-hopping
as courting couples kiss.

John Holloway

I'M IN LOVE

I'm in love, yes, I'm in love
With so many wonderful things!
Not only with the pure white dove,
But with all the birds with wings;
With their twittering songs and seagulls' shrills
That herald in all springs.

I'm in love, yes, I'm in love
With the trees and the fields I pass;
With the pansy, tulip and foxglove
And with every blade of grass.

I'm in love, yes, I'm in love
With the fairest rosy bower;
And I see God's hand above
In each and every flower.

I'm in love, yes, I'm in love
With the rivers, lakes and leas;
With all the wondrous waters,
Gushing down to the whole wide seas.

I'm in love, yes, I'm in love
With the whole of God's creation;
Showing His power and His love
To all and every nation.

I'm in love, yes, I'm in love
When I look upwards to the sky;
I'm in love, I'm in love,
I'm in love with a most
wonderful Guy!

Betty Wilson

GATHERING MUSHROOMS

The rising sun
Poked its roundness from Walker's Hill,
And dawn paraded over the green fields.
We moved forward
With renewed eagerness
In our search for the clumps of whiteness.
Cardy and the countryside was ours;
The day had not yet claimed it from us;
The stillness seemed to give us
A hold on our world.
I wanted it to stay like that,
But soon the basket
Would have claimed its quota,
And sounds and people
Would return
To take it all away:
And we'd be left
With our mushrooms
And an ordinary day.

Dennis S Nash

LOVE IS . . .

Love is a joyous friendship,
Two people sharing dreams,
Love is sitting by the fire,
With a hand to hold,
And having another person,
To be with when you're cold,
Love is not tearful,
Nor will it end in pain,
For the tears and the sorrow
Come when the love has gone away.

Jo Foreman

THE BUOYANT SEASON

At last - at last my heart cries out
The dark drab days of winter end
Throw off the duvet, windows opened wide
Let the soft winds sway the drapes as the
Clean air sweeps the room, and with it
Leaves the dust, the gloom,
Immersing me from head to toe -
Filling me with youth and foment.

This season initiates a palette wide
A spectrum range; an apparition of desire
I sense beginnings everywhere, in field
In forest, in garden plot, even in the
Market place, where *traders'* greetings
Sing not shout, more interest in their buyers' needs
Suddenly wishing to become a friend.

I take his hand and he takes mine
Together, a pebbled sea-wall climb
I feel him tremble as he stand so high
This moment must not rush by -
I clutch that hand to my body's side
Knowing that no words need pass
The tidings are so well conveyed
He too knows spring is here to stay.

Joan Richardson

THAT'S LIFE

She met him at the dance
And she was smitten.
They danced the night away
And she was lost.
He held her close
And called her 'Little kitten'
As he asked to take her home
In the last waltz.
Arms around each other
They strolled homeward,
And stopped sometimes
To kiss along the way;
They talked about themselves
Each to the other,
And blessed the fate
That let them meet this way.
He held her hand
And whispered that he loved her
(Well, love at first sight happens,
so they say.)
They wandered to her door
Then came the parting;
'I'll call tomorrow evening, eight o'clock.'
The next day she spent happily remembering,
And timed her preparations to the dot.
Then, putting on her coat,
She stood and waited:
I guess she's waiting still - for he forgot.

Beryl Laithwaite

THE GARDEN FETE

There's dear Mrs Frances all busy and bright
Unpacking her fine fare to look just right
With jars of jam, and pickles galore and
Many more pots all spread on the floor.

Jolly Miss Moore a plump little body
Who has worked so hard, now displays her hobby,
With jewellery fine, glinting every hue
All made so lovingly just for you.

Lots of good bargains to be found on the stalls,
Those mouth-watering cakes, I could eat them all.
Now, how about buying a book or two,
Some records or tapes, I could show you a few.

Oh there is our chairlady, all dressed up fine
To tell your fortunes, will she tell mine?
Side shows all busy there's so much to see
But soon the church clock chimes half past three.

Now all is packed up the money is spent
The gentlemen folk take down the big tent.
The teapots are empty all cups put away
Thank you for coming, we've had a good day.

Verna Warnock

MAID OF THE MORNING

As the fragrance of the roses,
fades with the sweet soft morning dew,
I'll speak your name within my heart
where I hold your love so true.

Your hair like flames of passion
flow within my floating mind,
your eyes like pools of crystal water
caress me from behind.

And just like the beat of my tender heart
I'll ache for your dear sweet lips on mine,
never more to part the love
that makes our lives divine.

The morning air is sweet my love,
I feel your presence near,
and though you're from another time
my love is still sincere.

Victor Robert Allen Day

SPRING'S ANNIVERSARY WALK

On the anniversary walk I go
Where the golden daffodils wave
As winds of spring softly blow,
Rustling through the willows,
Fluffy catkins falling listless,
        by the babbling brook.
Sound almost stilled by
        cawing nesting rooks.
Mossy bank where primroses grow galore
An ancient fort of hawthorns
Sanctuary for wild birds, overgrown unperturbed.
Planted by our forefathers years ago
Sleeping peacefully undisturbed.

Golden array of daffodils
Heads softly bowed as if in prayer
Captivating beauty beyond compare
April's ray of beauty another year

Another golden spring
Another golden anniversary.

Frances Gibson

IT DOESN'T MATTER HOW I TRY

I think it's time to let you go.
Let you loose from my mind;
My heart and my soul;
Let you loose from my dreams
And fantasies of you and I;
Let you loose from my spell,
That has been dwelled on you.

Now you are free and away from me,
'Cause that's how I want it to be.
'Cause no matter how I try,
To be around you and say 'Hi.'
I know I've got to let you go,
'Cause I'm wasting all my time.

And no matter what I do,
It still won't make you love me;
Like I've always loved you.
It doesn't matter how I try
To be myself and not to be shy.
You'll never learn to love me,
'Cause you just don't know how.

And even though I've said I've let you go.
You always enter my mind;
My heart and my soul,
'Cause boy I still love you so.
If you could just show me a sign,
To say that you want to be mine.

I'll be yours: till the end of time.

Maxine Easy

ECHOES OF SPRING

The fresh breath of a new day
Filters gently through my window
Flirting with the delicate curtains
Which perform a hypnotic dance
To intrigue and excite
And so the courtship continues.

I notice the distant hum of labouring bees
Accompanied by the soft symphony of tiny birds
Announcing the arrival of new life
Sustained by the rich glow of the warm sun.

The dark shadows, and icy blues of winter's cold embrace
Are erased instantly from my mind
As idle thoughts leave my head
Stretching across the shimmering surface of the garden
Wet with the morning dew
A thousand priceless jewels
Stare back with pride.

The thicket awakes from her dark slumber
And breaks the deafening silence
With an array of sounds.

I often hear the echoes of springs past
The crystal brook that carried our thoughts on thin rafts
As we watched from the safety of the bridge
The river bank's alive bedecked with flowers of rainbow colours
The sweet smell of spring
That still reminds me of you.

A timeless paradise
Where true love once flourished
A place to hide,
The perfect dream.

Peter Harris

SWEET HEARTS

When the cares of the world just seem to fly away
And just drift away on the breeze of a summer's day

When the burdens of the day are lifted from their heart
When there is contentment, when they are apart

When the cold mist of morning, is warm and bright
When the dark gloomy nights, look sunny and bright

When the days seem long and sometimes hard to bear
They long to run their fingers through each other's hair

In a kind of daze, they stroll without care
The hours drift past them, they seem so unaware

When the words that are spoken, set their ears ringing
The ache in their hearts makes them feel like singing

On meeting each other their eyes are a glaze
They kiss and embrace each other and walk in a daze

With this feeling of well-being for each other
They look into one another's eyes and call each other lover.

Roy Hunter

JOYS OF SPRING

What joy to look around each day,
Searching for awakening life in colourful display.
'Neath branches, whose buds are yet closed tight,
Then we find coltsfoot, snowdrop and aconite,
And leaves of later flowers can be found
Peeping through the wet cold ground
They promise warmth and perhaps some dryness
To welcome summer's flamboyant dress?

Alice Hall

SPRING IS IN THE AIR

Spring is in the air,
Oh, how jolly!
We can put away the tinsel
And the dried up holly.
We can open all the windows
To let the sunshine in,
Get out our gardening tools
Or go for a spin;
Change our winter woollies
For something cool and neat,
No more clumsy wellies,
We'll wear sandals on our feet.
Now it's cotton dresses
Silk ones if you're rich.
And no-one dares to murmur
I haven't got a stitch!
It's a pity I'm too ancient
To have a frolic in the hay
But life has compensations
Whatever time of day
With interesting hobbies,
And kindly friends galore,
We'll cast away care and gloom
And think of pleasant things
The garden's bright with flowers
And birds that love to sing.
The cuckoo will come calling
But I prefer the thrush
Who tries to sing his heart out
Atop the tallest bush

Ruby Button

MARCH CUCKOO

The first cuckoo in March I heard.
Oh what a welcome bird.
Now a warmth the sun will bring
That will make the birds all start to sing,
Spring is coming, it's round the corner,
It will now start to get warmer.

The end to all the winter frosts,
All the plants have not been lost,
We will plant some more,
While the swallows soar,
In the blue skies above,
Now is the time for love.

In spring it is said
That loving couples now should wed
While new life is beginning.
The birds are busy building
Their nests for young to come
Ready for the warmth of the summer's sun.

Janet Allwright

SPRING IN MY STEP!

A year has twelve months which consists of four seasons,
Each season a meaning and each meaning its reasons,
A Scottish winter, for example, is cold dreach and bleak,
It snows, we catch flu, then we're off work all that week.

We have summer and autumn, but in Scotland it's bonkers,
They're combined, weatherwise, except in autumn, leaves and conkers,
Summer is great, I love blue skies and sun,
Summer's for sunburn and holidays and fun.

Spring, the fourth season is when I'm full of fun,
It's the mid-time between winter till we reach summer sun,
Sunlit mornings and evenings a treat,
A shadow beside me at my feet.

Spring makes me feel good and makes me feel jolly,
I bring out the sunglasses and put away the brolly,
Spring makes us friendly and smile in the street,
Tipping our cap to people we meet.

Gillian Larkin

FIRST LOVE

Fingers touch and then draw back,
Move back and then clasp hands,
Beginnings of a first love,
Everyone understands,
Whispering secrets in pictures,
In the darkness of the rows,
Lights go on you break away,
Thinking that no-one knows,
Walking home in pouring rain,
Not caring if you get wet,
How long is it now? Two weeks,
Or more since the day you met.
First love is not forgotten,
It's in your heart to stay,
Then like a book it all unfolds,
When it's the autumn of your days.
You remember, and smile at your innocence,
You can't quite remember his name,
The first love you ever went out with
No others were ever the same.

E Hurcombe

LOVE

(Inspired by Sister Mercy)

True love is like the seasons
It blossoms like the spring
It brings joy and happiness
And the whole world seems to sing
The summer brings more passion
Like the heat of midsummer day
When all the world seems golden
And love is here to stay
Then comes the autumn
When passion seems to mellow
But love burns just as brightly
In a quiet and gentle way
The winter brings contentment
When hair has turned to grey
But love is just as beautiful
In a slow and tender way
And when the time is right
To start our lives anew
We know that our love
Will be forever true.

Joan Fowler

SPRING RETURNS

Spring is here once again,
Nature at its rebirth,
Flowers and trees budding,
Lambs, leaping and jumping.

Birds singing and nesting,
Everywhere around,
Fresh and new beginnings,
Spring is bursting forward.

Lighter and brighter days,
Sun and rain, together,
Warmer, with spring showers,
Greeting us daily, in the spring months.

Spring is here, once again,
Summer is not far away,
Longing for warmer days to come,
At the end of another spring,
Rushing forward, towards the summer days.

Diane Godbold

SPRING IS IN THE AIR

March winds and April showers
Bring forth May flowers
Yes, spring is here
Beauty near
Hearts a-beating, lambs abound
Romance and love in the air
Sun and kisses to be found
A lovely girl, so fresh and fair
A handsome boy, so tall and dark
Holding hands they strolled
In their eyes a hopeful spark
A perfect place to lie and cuddle
Amongst the sunshine heather
They rolled
Alas - just as - drat the weather
The rain came down to spoil
Hearts a-beating, just on the boil
Not to be, it all ended in a cosy huddle.

Dennis R Rowe

ONCE AGAIN THE EQUINOX

Spring has sprung, and winter's gone,
a new year bursts to life,
no longer darkened evenings,
the indoor TV life,
no need for saddened feelings,
the sun has warmed the earth,
Mother nature's labour is winter,
spring, her natural birth.
With all good things around us,
to touch, and feel, and smell,
once again the Equinox,
has measured her wondrous spell,
but fleeting for a moment,
stays, then waves goodbye,
as the sun climbs ever higher,
in a cloudless, turquoise sky.

Pat Judson

THE LILIES OF THE FIELD

Lords and ladies, arum flowers, upright, pure and fair
Cuckoo pints of cream and green arrayed beyond compare
Spiral trumpets heralding Easter's happy dawn
And sounding *alleluias* when the Lord of life is born
Lords and ladies, arum flowers, upright white and pure
Exceeding all majesty of Solomon's allure
Send out your psalms and praises to our great God above
Inspire us to continue life in faith and hope and love.
Lords and ladies, angel spires, flutes so pure and fair
Flowing with God's glory and delights beyond compare.

Monica Axford

THE SHORTEST SENTENCE

The shortest sentence I conceive,
That startles, comforts, often deceives,
A significant turn of phrase
Will at once a smile or a tear erase,
Can be turned and twisted
And used more ways
To pacify, hurt, or set ablaze
A human mind so full of need.
A sentence such can sow the seed
Of guilt of pride,
Alarm or shame,
Spoken seriously or in a game
Has such meaning to misconstrue
A short breathless utterance
'I love you.'

Tom Wilde

MARCH

March has caught the forest unawares
With her fleeting visit: trees hurry back
Into discarded clothes, and colour reappears
On naked winter limbs of sombre black.
Here and there, in the encroaching green,
Beeches take on a pinkish blur,
And signs of early blossom can be seen
Against the darker mass of forest fir.
In unseemly haste, keen honeysuckle weaves
Among the breaking leaves towards the sun,
Which, with its too-soon warmth, deceives
In letting us believe that spring's begun!

Bernard Parrott

DAWN LOVE

The early morning sun begins to show,
To make the daffodils and tulips grow.
The blackbirds' chorus at the start of dawn,
I wake with a smile and a happy yawn.
For soon I'll be with my one so dear,
To hold her close and very near.
She means more to me than anything,
My love to you my heart I bring.
A walk in the park and feed the ducks,
Enchanted by your angelic looks.
As a couple we'll always be hand in hand,
Emitting our love rays throughout the land.
Along the path of happiness for evermore,
We were meant for each other of that I'm sure.
So to my sweetheart, my darling, my friend,
My love for you I promise, will never end!

Jim Pullen

SPOKEN LOVE

While in half sleep, my love she spoke 'Tell me you love me dear'
My answer softly whispered back, and to her eye a tear
Should e'er you decide to part and wander here and there
I'd search the corners of the world to tell to you my care
I'd look the valley broad and wide, I'd climb the highest stone
I'd find you with my humble love, no matter where you roam
And when you found I'd come with haste and fall down at your side
And ask of you your loving grace, your arms for me to hide.
This much is how I love my dear, this much is how I care
For ever and a day my love, for you our love to share.

Terry Bowbrowicz

THE SEASONS OF LOVE

Cherry blossom drifting from the tree
Soft glances as we walk beneath its shade
The springtime of our love is here
And we rejoice with gladness, unafraid.

Bright poppies nodding thro' the corn
Summer sun gilds meadows, sea and sand
The world seems rosy, troubles few
As we tread softly, hand in hand.

Chill winds are blowing in those trees
Autumn frost has whitened leaf and grass
And suddenly the world has now gone cold
        Our love is past.

Winter's gloom descends in mist and rain
Spring, summer, autumn, past and gone
Warm sun gives way to grief and pain
        I am alone!

Audrey Crawford

A DAY LAST SPRING

I remember springtime, the sunshine and the flowers.
The time we sat beside a stream, to while away the hours
We spread a blanket on the grass, and you were by my side
I felt a surge of happiness, I'm sure I could not hide.
People that were passing by, looked at us and smiled.
The envy when they gazed at you, it really drove me wild
Your hot, and steamy, smouldering looks, mean everything to me,
'Cos you are all I want in life - my lovely cup of *tea.*

Norma C Crone

SPRING

I wonder is there is a thing
That is as welcome as the spring.
To cast aside those winter blues
Is like the pleasure of good news.

Love and romance are in the air
And youths pursue their maidens fair.
All of nature comes to life
The need to procreate is rife.

Spring's like a re-birth of our life
A time to be rid of winter's strife.
To plan ahead is our desire
Thoughts of holidays may transpire.

It's said we should ne'er cast a clout
That is until sweet May is out.
But in spring warmth when flowers bloom
We find it easy to cast off gloom.

New plants and flowers come to mind
We plan to try a different kind.
Seeds and seedlings must be fussed
To plan our gardens is a must.

As days grow longer and birds start to sing
We hear with pleasure their chorus ring.
And then I'm certain there's not a thing
That is as welcome as the spring.

Audrey Ann Hargreaves

LET FATE ROAM

Looked for hope, held onto the
dream of being free.
Others did not want to look,
I longed to see . . .

See beyond those four walls, and roam
further than the front door,
Lights faded out, and the media
told tales of more . . .

More than this suffering a
chance to escape,
So with a packed bag,
I stared in the face, *fate.*

A new college, a new home, a
left behind family, still.
Optimism ruled the stride of my
walk, and now if my eyes start to fill.

I look at what I've seen, and
what the mirror told me.
Now there's another door with
its own key.

Memories dead, but not buried, my
spirit free.

I look at my new room, my
new sketch,
I've closed that old door and opened the
next . . .

Christina Dagg

THE WONDER OF SPRING

Goodbye to winter, hello to spring,
The promise of new life makes my heart sing
As a baby is born from its mother's womb
So from the smallest seed emerges a beautiful bloom

Cascades of blossom grace the hedgerows
Alongside a meadow where a rushing stream flows.
Sticky buds form on horse chestnut trees
Whilst the birds build their nests, happy and free.

Tadpoles develop into frogs, what a feat!
Bees search for pollen for honey so sweet
Rabbits in warrens nurture their young
They produce many litters, new lives have begun.
With powder puff tails bobbing fluffy and white
A warning of danger in the twilight.

Beautiful butterflies, the warm weather brings
Intricate patterns on gossamer wings
Swallows and martins arrive for their stay
Also the cuckoo from lands far away.
Spring, the most wonderful time of the year.
The season of promise that I hold most dear.

Doreen E Kowalska

SPRING STEPS IN

There's a little leaf here
A blossom bud there
The sun is getting warmer
Spring is in the air.

The birds are singing
A more cheerful song
There's been the odd ant or two
Spring is moving along

It's grey in the morning
With a foggy layer
As the sun burns it off
Spring is getting nearer

The crows' nests abound
In the unleaved trees
That's the surest of signs
Spring is in the breeze.

R A Quinney

THE AWAKENING OF SPRING

At last the skies are blue again,
Fat buds are treacle sticky,
In spreading chestnut trees.
Little lambs' tails wagging in the breeze.
Pussy willows as soft and furry,
As the cat that lent its name.

Full babbling brook, from winter's rain,
Twinkling with spring diamonds,
Through welcome sunshine once again.
Yellow flowers once more abound,
Daffodils, crocus, celandine,
Starry forsythia butterfly broome.

Instinct tells the birds to breed.
Animals start to hurry and scurry,
Human hearts may skip a beat.
Lighter thoughts come to mind.

Try not to give your troubles heed,
Once more, it's good to be alive.

Irene S Hinton

GOD'S LOVE

The silence of Your love embraces me
I sense a smile.
An arm outstretched.
So still we sit
So still.
Each breath is wonder
Each thought delight and joy.
Unmarred by words
Unspoilt
O perfect love
Explode,
Drench us
Drown us
Deafen us to all our self-made noise
To all except
The silence of Your love.

Lynne Chitty

WHAT I WOULD NOT DO FOR HIM

On the wings of a dove I'd fly to him
Over oceans and sky for him
Into space and time for him
Oh what I would not do for him
Although I will always wait in my dreams for him
I know he will never be there for me
But there is always hope in eternity
Somewhere our spirits may meet
A blessing of love is so sweet
Jean Claude if you only knew
There is nothing on earth I would not do for you.

Stephanie Brown

AN OLD-FASHIONED SPRING

The snow had lain like a counterpane
Covering the sleeping earth.
On bush and tree expectantly
Mother Nature awaits to give birth
To her offspring, her offering,
And as the buds appear
Her attitude is gratitude
For the flowering of the year.

The rain drenches and slowly quenches
The thirsty earth, then it will fill
The dried up pond and stream beyond
To turn the wheel of the water mill.
Ducks at leisure with quacks of pleasure
Swim to their hearts' content
Fishes leap and take a peep
At this season which God has sent.

The soft wind blows and onward goes
Lifting the kite of the child
Clouds scurry and then seem to hurry
In case the wind grows wild
Daffodils swaying, children playing,
Old winter is on the run,
And the cuckoo now on yonder bough
Calls 'I'm back and the spring has come.'

Irene Peacher

IT'S SPRING

It's spring and the birds are all mating
They're going at it hell for leather
It's not that they need all that hassle with young
Just a good way to keep warm this weather.

It's spring and the crocus is peeping
It's bright coloured head to the sky
If it had any sense it would stay underground
And come out when it's warm, by and by.

It's spring and the little lambs gambol
Mid the primroses and the snowdrops
They'd be choked if they knew this was just a preamble
To turning them into lamb chops.

It's spring and the weather is balmy
Although not quite as barmy as folk
They strip off at the sight of a watery sun
And a frost-bitten wotsit's no joke.

It's spring and it soon will be summer
Then autumn when everything's frowsy
But whatever the season one thing is quite certain
The weather will always be lousy.

Joe Silver

A TOUCH OF SPRING

Spring dips the land in blazing yellow,
Tulips, white narcissus mellow,
Hyacinths, shrubs and heathers
Dancing like delicate feathers.
Swaying in the wind on green hills
All we can see are daffodils,

Dazzling our eyes with their gleam.

Airy music stirs sweet memories
When we kissed under the cherry trees
And pink blossoms touched my hair.
A chorus singing, love in the air,
A new awakening - then despair -
As you left me, the dreams of youth passed.
Tender green, a new love at last

With a softer breeze and hopeful dream.

Ingrid Riley

THE MAGIC OF SPRING

The woodpecker hammered, the bans were read,
A distant fox barked, we signed the pledge.
Two hearts will beat as one:
My story has just begun.

We walked through pine and silver birch,
Like the aisle in some forgotten church,
And ivy clung afraid to let go,
As if she loved her lover so.

Wild strawberry with its tiny white flower,
This season holds a magical power,
A sound of spring in the cuckoo we heard,
The echoing sound of that lonesome bird.

The blackthorn blossom like a bridal dress
With gentle breeze, the groom's caress,
The sound of a lark their wedding song,
And all the birds to join the throng.

Wild flowers to make the bride's bouquet,
As we remember that day in May,
The sweetest time from which dreams were made,
Walking hand in hand in that leafy glade.

June Coral Dye

BEAUTY REVEALED

Beauty, I have come to realise,
Is perceived by others in various guise,
Who can look on a field of rape,
Vivid, with a breath-taking beauty, and cannot fail to gape?
The acid of its yellowness, one can almost taste it,
What a crying pity others see, and not appreciate it,
Or, suddenly without prior warning,
A field of poppies massacred, whilst harvesting the corn in.

A dry and barren, desert land,
Retains still its beauty in dunes of sculptured sand,
And shells that litter, wave-washed beaches,
Each crafted and created in wonderful patterned pieces,
Every tree with its lacy green crest,
Appears the same, but is different from the rest.

Nature, it seems, delights in passing.
To us, these miracles of life, without asking,
Waterfalls from mountain peaks, gathering momentum,
Before tapering down into little creeks.

Who can deny the colour and spectrum, of each season,
Changing, unfolding, and adjusting temperature, for its own reason?
Wherever one looks, sheer beauty abounds,
Whether it be above, or under, the ground.
For, even below in caves, man or nature created,
I realise my smallness, my breath's held abated,
Of these glorious wonders, I could never be sated.

Our lives are too short to observe it all,
We are surrounded by beauty, let's conserve, not destroy it all.

June Hawkins

THE EFFECTS OF SPRING

It's a funny thing, but they say in spring
That a young man's fancies, turns to thoughts of love
When a man's been smitten, he's as silly as a kitten
And his eyes are like that of a dove.

In spring young birds cry, and lift their heads high
As for dinner they hungrily wait
And how I love the flowers and the soft spring showers
It's just the hayfever that I hate

When it's spring Down Under, and you hear the thunder
You know the blossoms might get wrecked
And when you see the birds come like thundering herds
You know your ripening fruit might get pecked

Coloured butterflies land, on the endless expand
Of masses of brilliant festoon
And every sunrise, heralds days of surprise
Which ends only all too soon

The magic of flowers as though they had powers
To capture your wondering heart
And the days you will gaze on the growing displays
And feel loss as the colours depart

Bees also cash in on the harvest of spring
Turning rich pollen into sweet honey
And butterflies flounce and kangaroos bounce
And so does the introduced bunny

Oh spring is so grand, in this blessed land
Where nature's displays are not mean
And through nature's all, in the large and the small
The hand of our God can be seen.

Marlene Peckham

SPRING IS IN THE AIR

As nature dons her spring attire,
Tempting us away from books and fire,
To start cleaning all of the house,
Decorating too, for man and his spouse.
Thoughts are turning to romance and love,
As the sun shines golden from above.
People appearing in garments so bright,
Thick winter clothing, now out of sight.
Our world looks so shiny and new,
Flowers and trees of every hue.
Blossoms falling in the scented air,
Baby animals with never a care.
Birds are bursting into joyous song,
After their languor all winter long.
Little lambs gambolling on dainty feet,
Men drilling fields, a deadline to meet.
Tender new shoots and fresh green leaves abound,
With hoards of bright flowers covering the ground.
Fluffy clouds scudding across the sky so blue,
Soft, gentle rain, maybe a rainbow or two.
The singing lark soars high into the air,
Heralding soon, glorious summer so fair.
Nature is now at its very best,
Waking from the long winter's rest.
As summer into autumn turn,
For spring once more, we'll surely yearn.

Sylvia A Smith

NEW LOVE

New love is as fresh as a new-born child
New love drives you seriously wild
New love is like the morning dew
Just because you are you
New love turns your world inside out
New love turns the world about
Sensuous and full of desire
Pins and needles
Love-making full of fire
New love
The ultimate desire
So tender and sweet
Those bodies so weak
Kissing and caressing
This new love
Goes on week after week
So hard to breathe
The urge the need
No time to feed
New love
This is what we all need
So take this love
With open hands
Show this world
And make a stand
True love lasts
Look back and gasp
This new love can
And will last.

Sylvia Haines

BLOSSOM

falls and lies as if from a
wedding feast
for other people's
happiness.

I must be one of the uninvited
because I do not know how
to be happy.

Bitterness is a cold wind
that drives right into summer.

But I am glad of spring:
of first opening leaves and
scent that fills the yard
behind the door.

For this beauty is not my work.

Effortlessly comes its noiseless moment
- not like my every effort to make a future
that now lies nailed in the past -

and I think of what the monk said:
'What opens is a sign to the will of God.'

We did not work to meet and walked out
like grains ground and watered,
flour clumping into dough.

Nor did we green the trees, or plan the leaves
to dart almost white grey plumes,
snapped a-dripping-silver snatched out
against the colding gloom.

And while we cannot rush happiness to happen,
neither let us stop, either, its glancing smile
and steady turn in the cycle of things,
turned in the hands of our gardening God.

Francis Etheredge

GARDEN WALK

Spring walked in the garden today,
There had been a shower of rain.
Upon the thirst-quenched, freshened grass,
It glistened as her feet trod new, green growth
And sprang to life where she did softly pass.

Bathed in fresh water
The many coloured flowers glowed,
A rainbow come to earth;
For love awoke them from their sleep,
Lifting laughing faces, spring's melodious mirth.

Rejoicing in the spring and love's new birth,
Among tumbled blossom
A bumble bee, gold and brown drank on the nectar,
As lazily he made his own erratic way,
And joined with the laughter.

High in the branches of an ancient pear tree,
A butterfly was born.
He stretched his wings and flew
Spring brightness here, glorious and free,
And my love strong and new.

A blackbird sang into the noon,
He soared into the sky.
I was content to stay, it was so pure, so sweet,
To listen to the fluting melody
Rise into the sky and mingle softly with the heat.

E C Mulligan

BUTTERFLIES

There is a butterfly that visits as many flowers as it can,
But then there is the one that simply goes from man to man,
If you're in the countryside, there are the exotic types of a
wonderful creation,
While the other *butterfly* is indulging in the closest possible relation.
Whereas the butterfly performs innocently, giving pleasure to us all,
The other one is no doubt popular, but is possibly heading for a fall.
We don't know how nature works, it's not influenced by wedding rings,
So even the butterfly is possibly deceiving us by its pretty
outstretched wings.
It may be just as promiscuous, we'll never know the facts,
For it's difficult to investigate and find out how it really acts.
We can use investigation regarding animal and insect activities,
In fact, it's assumed we gained our knowledge mainly from the
birds and bees.
We can still admire the miracles of nature, butterflies and all the rest,
But as for procreation we like to say 'I did it my way.'
And claim to be the *best.*

Reg Morris

SPRING IS IN THE AIR

Where are you hiding, spring
Behind winter's dark cloak, cold and thin?
Long-worn, threadbare, easy to break through,
And yet it seems an arduous task for you.

Arise, reveal your loveliness again,
Before your heir, summer, comes to reign,
Break forth with bud on trees long bare,
Impart to us your style so fair.

Let the fields breathe sweet, let the May appear,
Let the chaffinch sing - well upon our ear,
Primroses, daffodils, in the early morning dew,
Lambs, new birth, lift heart and spirit anew!

A young man's fancy, so they say,
Turns to thoughts of love when you come his way,
Let romance blossom like the hawthorn tree
And make us all feel fancy free!

Florence Scott

SPRING

The month of April says wake up arise the spring is here
The winter's frost and snows depart and Easter bells ring clear
Old mother nature doth unfold and kiss her friend the earth
And gardens which have quietly slept give out to beauteous birth
There's crocuses and daffodils and polyanthus too
And God has given each his own a pleasing sight to view
Forget-me-not with roving stem peep out with eyes of blue
And marigold with yellow face are there but not yet through
The sun has pushed its fiery head through clouds with silver sheen
It makes the countryside get dressed in brown and blue and green
The shrubs that once were bowed with snow are shooting now with ease
They're singing out with lilting song to their old friends the trees
And sleepy trees not yet awake are waiting for the call
Of nesting birds whose raucous cry is known to one and all
The mating birds their plumage bright are whistling out good cheer
And here's one place I love to be, ah yes now spring is here.

William Arthur Littleford

THE SPRINGS OF LOVE

Warm nights, the balmy air,
When I first saw you I would stop and stare.
Dog at heels and a purposeful stride,
A smiling face, eyes with secrets to hide.
I saw you many times after that,
Often we would stand, laugh and chat.
We became a pair, you taught me to live,
To love, and to be loved, to accept and to give.
We shared many things, our loves were the same,
This was a serious relationship, not just a game.
Springs, summers, winters, came and went,
We were happy in our little world, we were content.
Birthdays, anniversaries, we had them all
We worked, we played, oh how we played.
I loved you dearly, I would have been your slave.
Things started to falter, you needed space,
I had to accept this, find my own place.
I missed you, your laughter, the warmth of your love,
You were now my friend, life was very tough.
I would look back, remember everything of our two years,
The memories haunted me, there were tears and more tears.
The friendship has now gone, I never knew why.
I love you, you tall and silent man, of the secret eyes.

Christine Flory

LOVE, THE GREATEST GIFT

True love is something so special and rare -
A precious secret just two people share.
For her 'tis a time of memories sweet,
And a fulfilment of dreams to complete.
For him 'tis the time of manhood achieved
Through this gentle soul, who round his heart weaved
A magical spell, that bound them together
So strongly with love, that they could weather
All tempests of life, no matter how hard -
Nothing can touch them or leave their love scarred!
She thrills at the thought of having this boy
To share with forever, all sorrow and joy;
Be gently caressed by his loving hand;
To gaze into eyes she knows understand.
Just hearing his voice makes her heart swell with pride
To think that he chose her for his loving bride.
He said 'Love and cherish the rest of life through.'
Oh, there's nothing for him that she wouldn't do!
The words written here have poorly expressed
The greatest of gifts with which man is blest.
For this kind of love is something to treasure,
That two people share in infinite measure.

Natasha de Woronin

USURPED INNOCENCE

A pretty girl still in innocence,
Just in her sixteenth year,
Lay down upon the grass
Beneath the sky so clear.

She fell into a drowsy sleep
A tinker lad strolled by,
He lay down beside the girl
She awoke with breathless sigh,

In soft voice he spoke to her
She blushed at his frankness,
He continued his loving ways,
She begged him to cease his caresses.

Her thumping heart beat louder
She struggled faintly in his arms,
The lad's passion grew stronger
As he surveyed her youthful charms.

Equal passion now seized her,
Her heart pounding in rhythm,
In her responses to his actions,
She throbbed with every spasm.

She felt his total love for her
After all that they had done,
But when she smilingly awoke
Her tinker lover had gone.

Albert Wilson

JULIE'S PLACE

With hot moist and brazened skin,
They all knew on Keswick Common we'd bin.
The grass to shirt and blouse it sticks,
Ruffled hair and crushed cigarettes.
Careless but proud to love,
Another kiss from Julie's lips.
Red sun on our backs blue sky above,
Homeward bound it's kiss a stride.
From passing cars and bikes
Our secret we could not keep.
Be lovers all our lives we might,
But I ain't seen Julie since.
Finished up with egg on my face,
Because a secret I found out.
They all call Keswick Common, Julie's place.

Allen P Loveday

COUNTRYSIDE IN SUMMER

Imagine a country garden with the hollyhocks
and daisies high, cattle hushed at drowsy
afternoon, skylarks arrow-swift against the
summer sky, the orchard beckons me from tasks
that should be done, meadowsweet and gentian,
apple trees patterned by the noonday sun.
Corn stacks at harvest time in neat and tidy
lines, little tea-shops tucked away in leafy
winding lanes, village schools and ancient
inns tell of gentler times.

The country calls me once again whichever
sphere I roam Sussex downs and Wiltshire hills
Devon thatch and Cornish cove the church bell
ringing out tells me I am home.

Catherine Neale

CERASUS

Blossom-laden cherry tree
yields its stinking dandruff.

Eyes wide at three
behold the blizzard,
tissued fluff

cleaving selfish to each limb
like sun-bleached gnats
in springtime sky
dancing to the breeze's whim
they waver high
above my head
convulsing with refusal at
the proffered suit of red.

Relished icing sugar tree
soon forgotten
in this undressed state,

for pretty as its buds may be
you cannot *eat* the blossom.

Jo Riches

TREES

Sentinels and guardians of the wood,
Hiding place of Robin Hood,
Trees, that strange gigantic race,
Forming a canopy of lace.

Mighty oak and ash and lime,
Standing still throughout all time,
Watchers of the earth beneath,
Watchers of the earth we lease.

I wonder if the trees can cry,
When they look up at the sky,
Do they see the harm we do?
Will they die till they are few?

Mother Nature knows what's best,
She will survive all the rest,
The planet Earth will heal herself,
And trees will be her greatest wealth.

Jenny Smedley

NOAH

Noah ploughs the land with a broken plough
Behind an old horse, wise in the ways of how,
And where the plough should go as the earth turns
Over the ploughshare, while the birds sing and the sun burns.

Country-bred, Noah works harder for less
Than you'd think; blue eyes twinkle, but can you guess
What goes on behind them? Noah dreams dreams and scans
The horizon for rain; hold off for a day, Noah has plans.

Noah ploughs the land with a broken plough,
And smiles to think that green plants will grow
From work he has worked and seed he has planted,
Prayers he has prayed, that God has granted.

Noah's a good man, strong, yet gentle and kind,
He calls up the horse dreaming gone from his mind,
He furrows the ground straight and true, his eyes
On the land, his mind on his work, under clear skies.

Nick Spargo

OAK TREES

As I look westwards to the Malvern hills
Oak trees in scattered ranks predominate
Some form small woods but most old hedgerows mark
And visions of past history create.

Oak trees give permanence in changing times
As witness to each passing century.
Livestock may change, as also do the crops,
The oak tree stays and thus will always be.

The oak embodies English history,
Until the age of steel it formed her fleet
The heart of England's strength and fame abroad,
And furniture with which naught can complete.

Our future too continues to be marked
As by the planting of a sapling here
In Guarlford's churchyard, by the Bishop's spade
For future generations to revere.

This oak could live for nigh eight hundred years
Like one in Windsor Park, the oldest known.
Some others, although aged, have passed their prime
And now have hollow trunks, are broken down.

But most are etched in winter on the scene
Their branches clear in matching evenness.
In spring their outline softens as their buds
And leaves anticipate their summer dress.

Then it's in autumn when real beauty shows
Outlined in colour, red and green and gold
In massed profusion, every branch involved
Preparing us to meet the winter's cold.

Geoffrey Boaz

RUSTIC CHARMS

So we're in the middle of nowhere,
It's not recorded on the map.
But just smell the rural air,
Makes a change from *Watford Gap.*

Breathe in, till your lungs are full,
Go on, it'll do you no harm.
Experience the treasure of the green cathedral,
With all its rustic charm.

We've absconded from our urban closet,
And stepped into the great outdoors.
Left behind the grey deposit,
High-rise blocks and super megastores.

The only *McDonald* known round here,
Is that chap who's got the farm.
Stay off the cider, just drink the beer,
When down at the 'Ploughman's Arms.'

Here, horsepower's ruled for ages,
Though totally devoid of motorcars.
And trees can be seen without cages,
Or vandals' ugly chiselled scars.

Flowers grow wild and free,
Not in pots or herbaceous borders.
Whilst creatures dwell in field and tree,
Reliant not on human warders.

Paradise, is this pastoral shire,
A patchwork quilt of natural bliss.
A place to relax and even retire,
From that peace-engulfing metropolis.

Kevin Langwith

DOWN TO EARTH

The clouds descend from out of the sky and
Touch the tops of the hills and come right down to
The valleys below, making it impossible to proceed
Further. The rain descends too, and waters all the earth
With a touch of drizzle or a mighty thunderstorm.
The rainbow which starts from afar soars in the air but
Comes down to earth quite close. Up above soars the
Lark, singing with might and main but he, too,
Lands in the middle of some unknown field in some
Unknown spot where his mate lies, hatching her eggs.
The buzzard too, although he flies as high and
Gracefully, has to come down to earth for a meal and
Something to eat. O mother Earth! So solid and comforting
Underfoot, I feel you will never fail to support
The life dwelling on your surface.

T W Splitt

SEPTEMBER

The last sad mellow rays of summer
Fall lightly on the laden orchard bough,
Where age-darkened leaves hint of autumn colour
And ripened apples hang in full-blown glow,
Here yet the frantic bees still search for plunder
Unmindful of the season's dying breath,
While ill-tempered wasps gorge out their final hours
And butterflies flit headless to their death.

Soon no song of birds will break the melancholy stillness
As silent flocks pursue the lonely plough
Save the last russet-breasted chaffinch weeping softly
from the bough,

Soon he too will cease his mourning
The bees no more the air with humming fill,
Whilst butterflies become a sunlit memory
And earth will sleep in silent frost-bound still.

Robert Holding

SEASONS

Spring is here so fresh and green
Always remembered, once you've seen
Bluebells dancing in the wood
Their heavenly perfume smells so good

Primroses peeping through the grass
Stop and smell them as I pass
Wild pink blossom, violets too
Fields of clover soft with dew

Summer in the country now
See the piglets with the sow
Ripe red apples on the tree
Blackberries take home for tea

Autumn's here all bronze and gold
World of beauty to behold
Coloured leaves fall to the ground
Conkers, chestnuts all around

Winter's here in all her glory
Remind us of the Christmas story
All the world is sparkling white
The country's such a lovely sight

A Pearson

INFORMATION

We hope you have enjoyed reading this book - and that you will continue to enjoy it in the coming years.

If you like reading and writing poetry drop us a line, or give us a call, and we'll send you a free information pack.

Write to

Arrival Press Information
1-2 Wainman Road
Woodston
Peterborough
PE2 7BU